PENGUIN BOOKS

Information Overload

Dr David Lewis is a Chartered Psychologist, best-selling author and award-winning broadcaster. He is a fellow of both the International Stress Management Association and the Institute of Directors, a member of the Marketing Society, the Market Research Society and the Institute of Direct Marketing.

After studying medicine David Lewis became a magazine journalist, covering stories in Europe, the Middle East and Northern Ireland. It was his experience in Ireland that led to his decision to return to university to read psychology, obtaining his doctorate from the Department of Experimental Psychology at the University of Sussex. After lecturing there he left to set up his own research consultancy. A specialist in stress, his early books examined both stress and anxiety in children. Later, he began working with major multinational companies, such as British Airways, British Telecom and IBM, on staff develpment programmes. He is also a broadcaster and programme maker for both television and radio, and his series on the psychology of sporting partnerships for BBC radio won a prestigious Sony Award.

His recent books include *Ten-Minute Time and Stress Management* and *How to Get Your Message Across*. His latest book, *The Soul of the New Consumer*, will be published later this year.

INFORMATION OVERLOAD

Practical Strategies for Surviving in
Today's Workplace

David Lewis

PENGUIN BOOKS

PENGUIN BOOKS

Published by the Penguin Group
Penguin Books Ltd, 27 Wrights Lane, London w8 5tz, England
Penguin Putnam Inc., 375 Hudson Street, New York, New York 10014, USA
Penguin Books Australia Ltd, Ringwood, Victoria, Australia
Penguin Books Canada Ltd, 10 Alcorn Avenue, Toronto, Ontario, Canada m4v 3b2
Penguin Books (NZ) Ltd, Private Bag 102902, NSMC, Auckland, New Zealand

Penguin Books Ltd, Registered Offices: Harmondsworth, Middlesex, England

First published by Penguin Books 1999

1 3 5 7 9 10 8 6 4 2

Set in 9.5/12 pt PostScript Adobe Minion
Typeset by Rowland Phototypesetting Ltd, Bury St Edmunds, Suffolk
Made and printed in Great Britain by Clays Ltd, St Ives plc

Contents

Acknowledgements

My grateful thanks to Reuters for permission to use information gathered for their landmark report, 'Dying for Information'; Susan Pollock at Penguin; Roger Wells, who worked hard to make the book fluent and readable; Cynthia and Tony Hemming, who proof-read various drafts of the manuscript. Special thanks to Darren Bridger, who risked information overload in conducting the research for the book. Also for his help with generating concepts and writing some sections.

Introduction

'The world we have created today has problems which cannot be solved by thinking the way we thought when we created them.'
                                          Albert Einstein (1879–1955)

For someone like you, already burdened by handling large quantities of information on a daily basis, the prospect of adding thousands more words to your workload must appear daunting. So the question to ask before turning another page is: do I need to read this book at all?

Discover how helpful the practical strategies for dealing with overload which I describe in the following chapters will prove by ticking any statements that apply to you:

1. I find my working environment increasingly stressful.
2. I must make important decisions each day.
3. The market in which my organization operates is highly competitive.
4. I have to meet tight deadlines on a regular basis.
5. The number of deadlines is increasing.
6. The number of important decisions to make is increasing.
7. I receive a large amount of unsolicited information.
8. I need a lot of detailed information in order to do my job properly.
9. The amounts of information to be dealt with can only increase.
10. I need a lot of information to make important decisions.
11. I need a lot of information to keep pace with competitors.

12. I need a lot of information to understand constantly changing markets.
13. I waste a significant amount of time locating needed information.
14. I find it difficult to keep up with all the reading I need to do.
15. I often take work home and/or work longer hours in order to cope with overload.
16. I feel stressed by the amounts of information to be dealt with each day.
17. I am frequently interrupted when trying to concentrate on mentally demanding challenges.
18. I believe the amount of workplace stress caused by information overload can only get worse during the next few years.
19. I worry about making mistakes through failing to find relevant information.
20. My social life suffers because of the long hours I must work.

WHAT YOUR SCORE REVEALS

0–3: You currently appear to have few if any problems with information overload. Should your job change, however, the situation could also change, placing you in a more stressful environment. Although not essential to your present wellbeing or performance, the procedures described in this book could still prove invaluable by allowing you even greater mastery over workplace demands.

4–7: Although problems caused by information overload are still slight at present, you should keep a close eye on the situation. Any increase in workplace demands could easily put your health and performance at risk. Use the procedures I shall describe to maintain this healthy and productive state of affairs.

8–10: While still manageable, information overload is starting to pose a threat to your health and productivity. The procedures I shall describe in this book will enable you to bring information-related stress under control.

11–15: Your health, happiness and ability to work efficiently are threatened by information overload. The practical procedures described in this book will help you restore control to an increasingly untenable situation.

16+: You risk drowning in an ocean of information. Take immediate steps to master the practical procedures for handling information which I describe in this book.

HOW YOUR RESPONSES COMPARE

All but one of the questions above are based on a worldwide survey of information overload.

Conducted by Reuters,[1] it involved more than a thousand managers, in a variety of industries and sectors, from the UK, the USA and Pacific Asia. By comparing your responses with those given by executives around the world, you will be able to assess the extent to which they reflect your own experience.

1. *I find my working environment increasingly stressful.*

Four out of ten managers described their working environment as extremely stressful. Decisions, deadlines, tension with colleagues, long hours and a volatile marketplace combined to place executives under considerable mental and physical stress.

2. *I must make important decisions each day.*

World wide, seven out of ten managers reported that decision-making was a vital part of their working day. Women were slightly more likely than men to agree with the statement in the UK, significantly more in the USA and a smaller proportion in Singapore. In Australia and Hong Kong managers agreed to a significantly lesser extent, possibly reflecting a smaller role in decision-making responsibilities.

3. *The market in which my organization operates is highly competitive.*

Managers generally believe they operate in a highly competitive business environment, with a quarter strongly supporting this statement. People working in sales and marketing, PR and finance are especially likely to see their environment as unstable.

4. I have to meet tight deadlines on a regular basis.

Managers in the older western economies of the UK and the USA in particular are under pressure from tight deadlines, those in the Pacific Rim to a far lesser extent.

As one North American sales manager put it: 'There always seems to be a last-minute rush to get the job done – it's not always possible to prioritize your responsibilities, and then everyone is expected to pitch in.'

5. The number of deadlines is increasing.

For a variety of reasons, such as downsizing, heavier workloads and greater global competition, the workplace will be increasingly ruled by tight deadlines. The vast majority of managers (97 per cent) believe that pressures from deadlines will increase over the next two years.

6. The number of important decisions to make is increasing.

Sixty-eight per cent of managers agreed that demands made on them will increase significantly with higher levels of decision-making.

7. I receive a large amount of unsolicited information.

Across all countries and in all departments and industry sectors, managers report being swamped by unsolicited information. Around one-third receive 'enormous amounts'. Most at risk are middle and senior managers, with those in human resources being under greatest attack. Four out of ten managers in this sector say they receive 'huge' levels of unsolicited information.

8. *I need a lot of detailed information in order to do my job properly.*

Two-thirds of managers require a great deal of information, while a quarter need an 'enormous amount'.

9. *The amounts of information to be dealt with can only increase.*

More than half of American managers and four out of ten in the UK believe that information overload can only increase over the next two years. Women are more likely than men to cite the Internet as the main cause, while senior managers are most likely to see it as a key contributor to the build-up of Infoglut.

Nearly half of all managers world wide consider that the Internet will be a major contributor to information overload.

10. *I need a lot of information to make important decisions.*

A third of managers collect 'as much information as possible' for use in decision-making. As one UK financial services consultant put it: 'We are being forced to collect information just to keep our heads above water. It is simply a matter of survival.'

11. *I need a lot of information to keep pace with competitors.*

One in five managers believe that information is collected simply to keep up with colleagues. Managers in Hong Kong and Singapore are most likely to use information for this purpose, while one-third of junior managers in the USA recognize that information-gathering can be dictated by office politics.

12. *I need a lot of information to understand constantly changing markets.*

More than one-half of all managers, within all departments and sectors, world wide believe that very high levels of information are necessary in order to keep up with customers and competitors.

13. *I waste a significant amount of time locating needed information.*

Four out of ten senior managers are acutely aware of this source of stressful time-wasting.

14. *I find it difficult to keep up with all the reading I need to do.*

Almost half of all managers feel they are either often or very frequently unable to handle the volumes of information they receive.

15. *I often take work home and/or work longer hours in order to cope with overload.*

Almost one-half of the managers questioned said they quite often or very frequently stayed at work late or took work home with them so as to cope with the demands of information overload.

16. *I feel stressed by the amounts of information to be dealt with each day.*

The survey clearly identified information overload as a significant and serious threat to mental and physical health. One American human resources manager described how he 'became overwhelmed by the amount of information I was expected to digest – my doctor diagnosed that I was suffering from ME.'

A quarter said their stress was a direct result of information overload, while one in ten stated it was a frequent occurrence. Among the most commonly cited symptoms of such stress were loss of job satisfaction and tension with colleagues, which affected around two-thirds of all managers. Most at risk of health problems related to this stress were senior managers.

17. *I am frequently interrupted when trying to concentrate on mentally demanding challenges.*

Although this question was not included in the Reuters survey, other research[2] suggests that the average UK executive deals with 190 messages a day and that four out of ten managers are interrupted at least once every ten minutes. Interruptions typically include 48 telephone calls, 23 e-mails, 20 letters, 15 internal mail messages, 13 Post-it notes, 12 message slips, 11 voice mails, 11 faxes, 8 mobile phone calls, 3 express mail deliveries, 2 pager messages and 2 courier deliveries.

18. *I believe the amount of workplace stress caused by information overload can only get worse during the next few years.*

Almost two-thirds of managers predict that the future will be even more stressful than the present, with middle managers likely to be worst affected. They predict significant increases in decision-making and tight deadlines.

19. *I worry about making mistakes through failing to find relevant information.*

This emerged as a serious concern for a majority of managers. As one telecommunications executive in Singapore explained, 'It's gotten to a stage where you cannot come to a decision without worrying that someone might have more information than you and could make your decision look wrong.'

20. *My social life suffers because of the long hours I must work.*

The 'leisure society' so confidently predicted by many only a few years ago now seems an impossible dream to most managers and professionals.

Workloads are relentlessly increasing while leisure time is constantly being chipped away. Sixty per cent of managers world wide say they are too tired for leisure activities as a direct result of dealing with information overload, while a similar proportion claim their personal relationships suffer for the same reason. Half blame their ill-health on having to deal with excessive information.

In the Reuters report, *Dying for Information*, I wrote: 'What this . . . makes crystal clear is that finding ways of dealing with the information burden is now one of the most urgent world-wide challenges facing business. For unless we can discover ways of staying afloat amidst the surging torrents of information we may end up drowning in them!'

While we cannot stop or even slow down the flood of facts and figures we have to deal with, mental strategies exist that will allow us to swim against the tide more easily and effortlessly.

Abraham Lincoln remarked that, if he had nine hours to cut down some trees, he would spend the first six hours sharpening his axe.

It is in this spirit of intellectual axe-sharpening that I suggest you approach the procedures for dealing more effectively with the dangers of information overload that I shall be describing in the following chapters.

1 The Menace of Information Overload

> 'The first signs of a massive cultural mutation are becoming evident. In a society already plagued by stress-related illnesses from hypertension to cancer, techno stress may be the most crucial disease we ever have to face.'
>
> Craig Brod, *Techno Stress: The Human Cost of the Computer Revolution*

During the past few years it has become increasingly clear that constantly dealing with large amounts of information, frequently against tight deadlines, poses a significant threat to health and happiness. To understand the kind of pressures that are now widespread in many organizations, let's look at a typical day as it used to be experienced by Chris, one of my clients. (Although I have chosen a man to describe the threat now facing millions of white-collar workers around the world, the victim could just as easily have been a woman.) Until recently a senior manager in the human resources department of a major pharmaceutical company, some months ago Chris suffered a breakdown. After more than twelve weeks off work, he managed to get another job at a lower salary but in a less stressful environment.

A DAY IN THE LIFE OF CHRIS

As usual, Chris arrives at his office early, in the hope of putting in some uninterrupted work on an important and urgently needed report. Even first thing in the day, he finds his in-tray filled with documents, reports and memos. Some have been put there during the previous night, others represent uncompleted tasks from the previous day.

Gloomily, he sifts through the technical papers, minutes of recent meetings, product evaluations, interdepartmental reports, letters and fax messages, then he places them in one of three piles according to their urgency. With luck he will be able to deal with the most urgent during the day. The rest must await their turn, this year, next year, sometime, never!

Turning on his computer, Chris finds almost a hundred e-mail messages awaiting his attention. Being a multinational, his company works round the clock. Somewhere in the world there are always people at their desks, piling up the demands on those trying to catch up on their sleep.

Already weary and dispirited, Chris fetches a black coffee and settles down to work. He hasn't been sleeping well in recent months, dropping off in front of the television but feeling wide awake the second his head hits the pillow. Once in bed, he tosses and turns until the small hours, going over the previous day's events again and again in his mind, worrying what mistakes he might have made, dreading the challenges of the morning ahead.

In the past he had been able to unburden himself to his wife but, since he started arriving home so late and going in to the office so early, their relationship has started to unwind. Now they exchange only a few words each day, and these are mainly about domestic arrangements. At the weekends he feels too tired to join in the family activities and hasn't felt like playing with his two young children for months. The previous Saturday he was supposed to attend his ten-year-old son's sports day, until an emergency at the office forced him to cancel. He is painfully aware just how hurt and upset both his son and his wife had been about that.

By the time Chris has dealt with the urgent correspondence and responded to priority e-mails, the office is filling up and phones are starting to ring. For the next few hours he struggles to complete his report, in the face of constant interruptions from telephone calls, e-mails, and requests for assistance. After each distraction Chris finds himself wasting more time as he refocuses on the task at hand.

Over a snatched lunch of sandwiches and coffee, eaten at his desk, he struggles to catch up with his reading of technical papers and magazine articles concerning his company. But his mind is so full of other problems and concerns that he finds it hard to concentrate on the text; the words seem to flow into a meaningless blur, with nothing making much sense. Never a fast reader, he finds trying to understand and learn complex new information under such pressure all but impossible.

Throughout the day he has to take important decisions and solve a variety of problems, many carrying serious implications for himself and his company. After each one, Chris worries whether he has taken account of all the relevant information. Suppose a rival company is better informed and so able to make smarter decisions or come up with more efficient solutions?

By the end of the day, head aching, stomach queasy from the grabbed lunch and muscles cramped from sitting too long behind his desk, Chris feels both exhausted and deeply frustrated.

Despite all his hard work, little appears to have been accomplished; so much remains to be done that, once again, he will either have to stay late or take work home. Either way, this means more disruption to his private life, more rows with his partner and further guilt at not spending time with his children.

Chris is drowning in an ocean of information, and increasing numbers of people in business and the professions know exactly how he feels. In Europe, the USA and Pacific Asia, where more than half the Gross National Product is now derived from the labours of information workers, almost all managers and professionals are now at some degree of risk. Like the Red Queen in *Through the Looking-Glass*, they are having to run faster and faster just to stay in the same place.[1]

Perhaps you are one of them?

So widespread is the problem posed by overload that a new word, 'infoglut', has been coined to describe it. This ugly but apposite word refers to the torrents of information, much of it irrelevant, that currently clog up the arteries of business. If it continues long enough, the pressure of infoglut can bring on a major threat to mental and physical wellbeing, IFS or Information Fatigue Syndrome.

WHAT IS INFORMATION FATIGUE SYNDROME?

The main feature of IFS is, of course, fatigue – not the perfectly normal and natural weariness everyone experiences after a hard day's work but a deep, numbing exhaustion which even a night's rest fails to relieve. It is a chronic debility of mind and body that leads to an increasing inability to:

- concentrate
- prioritize
- distinguish between relevant and irrelevant information
- make sense of unfamiliar material
- cope with intellectual challenges
- maintain your confidence and motivation
- make up your mind over complex issues
- reach decisions and solve challenging problems.

Before very long, failures at work result in additional and related problems in health and one's personal life. Sleep is disturbed and rising stress levels may be implicated in physical ill-health, including heart disease, high blood pressure, diabetes, and an increased risk of going down with minor infections such as colds and flu. Longer hours at work also put personal relationships in jeopardy, leading to depression, anxiety and panic attacks.

ARE YOU AT RISK FROM IFS?

The questionnaire below will enable you to compare your current levels of stress with the average for your occupation. I suggest you repeat the test every few months, or at any time when there are significant changes in your working situation.

Complete the assessment by selecting the most appropriate response to each of the 15 questions and scoring as follows:

Response	Score
Does not apply	0
Never	1
Rarely	2
Sometimes	3
Rather often	4
Nearly all the time	5

How Often Do You:

1. find yourself without the information needed to carry out all the responsibilities placed on you?
2. have difficulty getting hold of facts and figures required to do your job efficiently?
3. feel unsure about the scope and responsibilities of your job?
4. have so much information to deal with that it is impossible to complete all the tasks demanded of you during a normal working day?
5. lack the authority to handle information in the way you regard as the most efficient and effective?
6. not really know whether your decisions and solutions are the best possible ones?
7. worry about your decisions that will affect the lives of those working with you?
8. fail to influence a superior's decisions or actions even though these affect you?
9. find that the mental overload caused by your job interferes with your family life?
10. believe your job requires you to do things against your better judgement?
11. feel uncertain what your colleagues or superiors expect of you?
12. find that the volume of work makes it impossible to do those tasks as well as you would like?
13. consider yourself insufficiently informed to cope with the demands of your job?
14. worry whether you have missed some piece of vital information?
15. feel unclear as to the opportunities for promotion or advancement within your job?

How to Score

1. Total your score.
2. Subtract from 15 any questions you scored as 0 (because they did

not apply). For example, if you scored zero on six questions, this would leave a total of 9 (15–6) relevant questions.
3. Divide your final score by the number of relevant questions.
4. Compare this with the average for your occupation on the chart below.

Example:

    1. Total score = 59
    2. Three questions scored zero because they did not apply: 15–3 = 12
    3. IFS score = 59÷12 = 4.9.
    As you can see from the chart below, such a score would indicate a very high risk of IFS.

SCORE CHART

Your occupation	Your risk of suffering from IFS		
	Normal	Moderate	High
Professional, technical	2.0	2.1–3.4	3.5+
Managerial	1.8	1.9–3.2	3.3+

If your score is average, or even slightly below average, for your occupation, it suggests that stress created by handling information overload is not causing problems at present. Of course, it is still possible to experience high levels of acute stress in specific situations.

Within organizations, overload contributes to the 'productivity paradox' surrounding the ever-increasing use of computers. For more than two decades, companies in the USA and Europe have been making huge investments in information technology in the confident expectation that this would dramatically increase productivity. Yet, during the same period, productivity growth has actually been declining. In the USA, the output per worker has slowed from an average post-war gain of 3.2 per cent per year to a mere 1.2 per cent between 1979 and 1994.

Figures for multifactor productivity, a measure of how much output is produced from a given set of inputs, show a similar decrease. Over the past twenty-five years, this has grown by only around 0.3 per cent per year from 1973 to 1994, compared with 2.2 per cent during the previous quarter-century. 'The question is inescapable,' says *Fortune* writer Matt Siegel. 'Are computers *not* making business more productive? Could they actually be hurting?'[2]

While the economic jury is still out on the 'productivity paradox', there is no doubt that the relationship between human beings and computers is far less clearly beneficial than many believe.

Where computers excel is in storing, retrieving and analysing virtually unlimited quantities of data with unrivalled speed and precision. There is, however, a danger of endowing them with powers they do not, and may never, possess. As computer writer Stephen Alsop remarks, 'The nirvana of software that helps us think better is a fantasy.'[3]

Easier access to information also poses problems for some organizations in that the value of commercial knowledge depends on the amount of time and effort invested in obtaining it. The value of information is related directly to the extent to which it is unique and can be used for personal, professional or commercial benefit. Information which is easily come by and may be obtained by anyone is, as a general rule, commercially worthless.

Fortunately, there is a wide variety of practical ways in which the stress of overload may be reduced, with significant benefits both to individuals and to the organizations they represent.

The purpose of this book is to describe these procedures and to demonstrate how they can help you survive and prosper in a world in which infoglut has become an established fact of life.

SUMMARY

- In this chapter I have explained some of the reasons why information overload has arisen and why bringing it under control should be a top priority, both for individuals and for organizations.
- Chronic overload poses a threat to mental and physical health, leading to a loss of motivation and a decline in productivity.

● For organizations, IFS has a significantly adverse effect on the bottom line, resulting in worse rather than better decisions, confusion and declining morale.

2 Mind Traps: Nine Overload Errors You Must Avoid

> 'In the past, information was the real bottleneck, so any im-
> provement in information would lead to an improvement in
> thinking and in the quality of decisions. Information access and
> handling [by computers] have widened that bottleneck. So we
> move on to the next bottleneck. This is thinking. What do we
> do with the information? Most people in business and govern-
> ment have not fully faced that change.'
>
> Dr Edward De Bono, *Parallel Thinking*

Glance around your office. Chances are, the desks and filing cabinets are at risk of being submerged beneath an ever-rising tide of information. Files, memos, reports, faxes, manuals, books, journals, surveys, inventories, projections, business plans, printouts, magazines and newspapers are crammed into every corner and overflow from in-trays.

Turn your computer on, and dozens – perhaps hundreds – of e-mail messages may demand your urgent attention. Log on to the Internet and, almost instantly, more knowledge becomes available to you than your parents could have accessed in their entire lifetime.

Over the past twenty years the growth in information has reached a point when virtually unlimited knowledge is no further than a mouse-click away on the Internet.

HOW INFORMATION GREW AND GREW

For thousands of years, written texts, whether carved in stone or penned on scrolls, were humankind's only way of preserving and communicating information. The need for copying by hand made producing documents a slow, laborious and error-prone affair and the lack of an index made finding required information equally difficult. This is why educated Greeks developed some of the powerful memory techniques that I describe in Chapter Six. The mass-production and dissemination of written material became possible only with the invention of the printing press by Johannes Gutenberg, a Strasbourg goldsmith, in 1439.

The next revolution occurred in 1947, when Claude Shannon, an engineer at the Massachusetts Institute of Technology, discovered that information could be broken down into basic building-blocks that he called 'bits' (from *bi*nary dig*its*). In this form they could be stored, manipulated and communicated with greater ease and accuracy than ever before.

The final step in the universal distribution of information came, twenty years later in 1969, with the development of the Internet from four linked computers. The 'net' has grown to embrace over 30 million computers in more than sixty countries, and it is believed to contain in excess of 100 million pages of information, although nobody actually knows – or can ever know – just how large it really is. The Internet is thought to be expanding at the rate of 200,000 extra pages of information daily, and by the year 2000 it could link as many as a billion users.[1]

The Internet has radically transformed our relationship with information in two specific ways: first, in the speed at which it can be communicated and, secondly, by significantly increasing the scope for making new discoveries by linking together disparate items of information.

All this information creates a delicate web that permeates entire business organizations; it is the raw material on which personal, professional and commercial success depends.

At first blush this may seem like an ideal situation, one in which nobody need ever be starved for essential information when making decisions or solving problems. Yet studies suggest that the sheer volume of available material, combined with tight deadlines, time constraints and the difficulty of accessing relevant facts and figures, means that most of it remains unused and unread.

This inability to track down all available information is in itself an additional source of stress for many managers. At the back of their mind lurks the fear that competitors, by searching more cleverly and diligently, will be able to discover new facts or figures that will give them the winning edge. The more information that is available and the more volatile the markets in which they operate, the greater this concern becomes.

One damaging consequence of this fear of missing out on something vital is that the mere collection of data becomes confused with the accumulation of knowledge. And this brings us to the first of the nine mind traps that create unnecessary stress and lead to avoidable errors of judgement.

MIND TRAP ONE – MISTAKING DATA FOR KNOWLEDGE

In *Information Anxiety*, author Richard Wurman points out that: 'The great information age is really an explosion of non-information; it is an explosion of data. To deal with the increasing onslaught of data, it is imperative to distinguish between data and information. Information must be that which leads to understanding.'[2]

Data, the plural form of *datum*, 'that which is given', is often defined as a set of discrete, objective representations of facts, concepts or instructions. In the context of 'overload', a more useful way of looking at data is as stimuli which bring about electrochemical changes in our brain. Data, to paraphrase a comment of anthropologist Gregory Bateson, are the 'differences which make a difference'.[3]

As an example, consider how you are reading this book.

Light reflected from the pages is causing the lenses in your eyes to focus the images of letters and words on to the retinas. This stimulates changes in light-sensitive cells (rods and cones), which, in turn, produce a cascade of changes in the cells forming the optic pathway, resulting in changes in the various regions of the brain concerned with vision. This enables you to make sense of what is written.

'Your brain changes,' says neurologist Stephen Grossberg. 'It changes a little bit every time you see an image or hear a sound or feel a surface or taste a flavour or walk a new ground. Everything you sense changes your brain. Your brain measures things and those things change your brain. It learns new changes and forgets or unlearns old changes. A single photon of light changes your brain. TV ads and movies and books and talks and jingles and all the stuff that your mind eats change your brain. It changes right now as you read this.'[4]

To bring about these changes, your brain has to expend energy and it is this, eventually, that leads to mental fatigue; in time, it can lead to a loss of concentration and an inability to think clearly or rationally.

One of the strategies the brain uses to reduce fatigue is to pay greater attention to anything that is new, different or unusual in our surroundings, while taking less notice of things that remain unchanged.

You can test this for yourself by extending your arms sideways, parallel to the ground, at shoulder height, and keeping your fingers still. After a few moments the fingers will become almost invisible. Now wiggle them, and awareness of them instantly returns.

In a business environment, this can easily lead to the first of our nine mind traps. Our attraction for the unfamiliar causes us to pay greater attention to what is unfamiliar or unusual; as a result, we may be beguiled into decisions that make no sense in terms of a company's overall business strategy, as we discard the known in favour of something new, not because the latter is necessarily better but because it appears to be more interesting and exciting.

How to Avoid This Trap

Without ever casually dismissing a new idea simply because of its unfamiliarity, beware of being led astray by novelty for the sake of it. In a society constantly exhorted by advertising to favour the 'new', the 'improved' or the 'latest', it is only natural to believe that something of breathtaking originality must be superior to what has gone before.

Keep your feet firmly on the ground, perhaps bearing in mind the story of the salesman who tried to persuade a famous firm of piano-makers to switch from brass pegs for holding the piano wire to lighter aluminium ones.

'I'm quite prepared to give them a fair trial,' the managing director replied. 'If they prove as satisfactory as brass, we shall certainly consider changing over to them.'

'Excellent,' replied the delighted salesman. 'When shall I come back for your answer?'

'Oh, in about a hundred years,' was the bland response!

MIND TRAP TWO – GATHERING EXCESSIVE DATA

Confronted by access to huge quantities of data, some companies adopt the view once espoused by the East German secret police: you cannot ever know too much about anything. Touring their headquarters after the Berlin wall had come down, citizens of the former DDR were astonished by the vast amounts of information collected on every citizen. Bulging dossiers included scraps of gossip and tit-bits of the most trivial kind from tens of thousands of petty officials and informers. Yet all this effort by the faceless bureaucrats signified nothing; it merely reflected a fanatical obsession with data-collection and a belief that, by gathering enough of it, knowledge relevant to the security of the DDR would automatically emerge.

Much the same mistaken obsession can rule in many commercial organizations. 'Firms sometimes pile up data because it is factual and therefore creates an illusion of scientific accuracy,' comment leading management consultants Thomas Davenport and Laurence Prusak. 'Gather enough data, the argument goes, and objectively correct decisions will automatically suggest themselves.'[5]

There are two reasons why such assumptions are dangerously false: first, having too much data actually makes it far harder to find what you really need to know in order to separate the dross from the nuggets of gold; secondly, data in itself is without any meaning, it cannot tell you how to think, which solutions to problems will work and which are doomed to fail, and it offers no judgements and provides no interpretation or any basis for action.

As computer specialist Michael Dertouzos points out: 'With a billion or so interconnected computers around within a decade, and with each computer carrying a few thousand to a few million bits of information, we will be surrounded by a mountain of data – somewhere between a trillion and a quadrillion files, programs, notes, lists, and other material. For many of us, most of it will be a mountain of info-junk with zero value. All we want are the few nuggets that help us in the pursuit of our own desires and goals.'[6]

How to Avoid This Trap

Never allow yourself to be carried away by the misleading assurance that data often provides. This applies especially to statistics, a source of more errors and false conclusions than almost any other type of supposedly 'hard data'. As Benjamin Disraeli is said to have remarked, 'There are lies, damned lies and statistics.'

Another source of mistakes is jargon, the use of unnecessarily technical expressions and long-winded words whose purpose is to conceal rather than enlighten. Never make assumptions about data, and always double-check that you really understand what the facts and figures mean. This is not to say that data is unimportant, because of course it is not. Data is the raw material out of which first information and subsequently knowledge can be created.

Information has been defined by Peter Drucker as 'data endowed with relevance and purpose'.[7] But in the act of endowing data with that necessary relevance and purpose, we risk falling into two further mind traps.

MIND TRAP THREE: SEEING WHAT IS NOT REALLY THERE

Because our brain looks for patterns, we risk 'discovering' information where none exists. Shakespeare illustrates this point perfectly in an exchange between Hamlet and Polonius, his Lord Chamberlain:

HAMLET: Do you see yonder cloud that's almost in shape of a camel?
POLONIUS: By the mass, and 'tis like a camel indeed.
HAMLET: Methinks it is like a weasel.
POLONIUS: It is backed like a weasel.
HAMLET: Or like a whale?
POLONIUS: Very like a whale.

We have probably all shared a similar experience of appearing to see shapes and forms where none actually exists. Information overload increases this danger by producing so much information that the chance of confusing random associations with cause and effect or perceiving significant patterns where none exists increases enormously.

An example was the media hype generated by *The Bible Code*, a book which claimed to have discovered all kinds of predictions, omens and warnings by means of computer analysis of the Hebrew text. This caused a great deal of excitement and astonishment until a computer expert found exactly the same kind of forecasts and predictions in a number of other texts, including Herman Melville's *Moby Dick*.

In business, wishful thinking can cause even experienced and highly educated managers to extract facts and figures from data that do not really exist and then selectively take note of further evidence in support of their mistaken beliefs, while rejecting anything that contradicts them. The more data you have and the less time you have to analyse it, the greater the risk of making unsupportable inferences and arriving at false conclusions.

How to Avoid This Trap

Safeguard yourself by constantly questioning all assumptions arising from the data, especially where the issues are complex. Beware of confusing 'correlations', in which events occur together, with causation. Around springtime, storks appear in Swiss villages, and Swiss women give birth to babies. These events are highly correlated, but no one over the age of five surely believes that they are linked causally.

MIND TRAP FOUR: BEING INFLUENCED WITHOUT REALIZING IT

The way in which we interpret information can be significantly influenced by something seen, heard, or even smelt below the level of awareness. An example of this is known as the 'cocktail party' effect. Imagine you are at such a party and are chatting with another guest. Although you are surrounded by people, engaged in their own lively conversations, it is quite easy to shut out the surrounding chatter and concentrate on what the other person is saying to you. Without being aware of the fact, you are simultaneously listening in on other conversations. If someone mentions your name, your attention is immediately drawn to that individual.

When evaluating information you could equally easily be influenced, without realizing it, by something seen or heard below the level of awareness.

How to Avoid This Trap

Safeguard yourself against unconscious biases by trying, whenever possible, to test your assumptions by means of experiments or through direct experience. A little practical testing is often worth more than a mountain of theoretical data. The Greek philosopher Plato, for example, believed that men and women had different numbers of teeth. As Bertrand Russell commented, this error could easily have been avoided by the simple expedient of opening Mrs Plato's mouth and counting her teeth.

MIND TRAP FIVE: FILLING IN GAPS WITH INVENTED MEMORIES

When something is lacking in our recollection, memory often provides false but convincing data to fill the gap, by the process known to psychologists as 'confabulation'. Convincing but utterly false memories can create serious difficulties for managers and professionals who take important decisions on what appear to be clear recollections, only to discover that they have been misleading themselves.

An excellent example of this innocent confusion occurred during a lecture on policing given by the late Fred Inbau, a criminologist at North-Western University at Evanston near Chicago. In the middle of his class, an armed robber burst in and mugged the professor, before fleeing with his briefcase. Immediately after the event Inbau asked his students to describe the assailant. Not surprisingly, they all had a vivid recollection of the amazing event. The problem was: they all had *different* vivid recollections! Some insisted he was fat, while others were equally certain he was thin; some claimed he wore glasses, others that he did not. His height was variously reported as anything from 1.65 metres to 1.95 metres. His hair was either bleached blond or mousy or jet black. He had been wearing a denim shirt and blue jeans or a leather jacket and brown corduroys.

The 'mugging' was, of course, a set-up, intended by Professor Inbau to demonstrate the fallibility of eye-witness testimony. Despite the very different accounts of what had happened, each student was convinced that he or she had got it right; their recollections were accurate, while all the others had been honestly mistaken. As Alexander Pope so perceptively remarked in his *Essay on Criticism*:

> 'Tis with our judgements as our watches, none
> Go just alike, yet each believes his own.

How to Avoid This Trap

This does not mean that you should despair of using your memory, nor should you tell yourself you have a rotten one or dismiss your ability to retain and recall large amounts of information. As I shall explain in Chapter Six, powerful methods exist to enhance the speed and accuracy of recollections. What we must always bear in mind, however, is that recall unsupported by any other evidence should be treated with caution. Even checking with colleagues who were present when the information was first discussed may not be sufficient to prevent errors.

The only safeguard against 'confabulation' and similar sources of honest mistakes is by reference, whenever possible, to contemporary sources, by means of written, audio or video recordings.

MIND TRAP SIX: OLD KNOWLEDGE BLOCKS OUT NEW

Information organized into a coherent whole and then learnt is transformed into personal knowledge. This learning is a three-step process, as is shown in the table below.

How Knowledge Is Acquired

TO **FROM**	Unconscious Ignorance	Conscious Ignorance	Conscious Knowledge	Unconscious Knowledge
Unconscious Ignorance	XXXXXXX	**Awareness**	XXXXXXX	XXXXXXX
Conscious Ignorance	Inappropri-ateness	XXXXXXX	**Learning**	XXXXXXX
Conscious Knowledge	Inactivity (boredom)	Instability	XXXXXXX	**Practice**
Unconscious Knowledge	Inactivity (forgotten)	Inactivity (remembered)	Indifference	**Use**

The Learning Ladder

At the start, an individual is in a state of **Unconscious Ignorance**. The realization that there is important knowledge to be acquired leads to **Conscious Ignorance**. Study and instruction produce **Conscious Knowledge**, while familiarity and repetition lead to **Unconscious Knowledge**.

The blanked-out diagonal elements indicate activities that do not bring about any changes in an individual's state of mind. The first three represent wasted effort, while the fourth, 'Use', maintains the same level of knowledge.

Of the six entries that form the upper right triangle, three form a ladder taking us from *awareness* that there is something worth knowing, through *learning* to *practice*.

One example of climbing this ladder is learning to use a computer. At first an individual is not even aware (Unconscious Ignorance) of the value which this equipment may offer in his or her line of work. Made aware of the machine's possibility (Conscious Ignorance), the person sets out to learn how to use it. After a while he or she becomes quite adept (Conscious Knowledge) in its use. But only after lengthy practice and experience (Unconscious Knowledge) will that individual be able to concentrate entirely on the task for which the computer is being used, be it data analysis, word processing or whatever, without having to think about which key to strike next.

Although essential for efficient working, in a world where information is rapidly changing, Unconscious Knowledge can result in two different mind traps, either of which may have devastating consequences.

MIND TRAP SEVEN: RESISTANCE TO CHANGE

Anthropologist Ashley Montagu has coined the word 'psychosclerosis', or a 'hardening of the categories', to describe the process by which we become more and more certain of less and less. Just as atherosclerosis, or hardening of the arteries, can destroy the body, so too can psychosclerosis harden the mind to a point where thinking becomes dogmatic and inflexible. We are no longer open to new ideas or insights; anything that challenges or contradicts our established way of looking at problems or decisions is dismissed, often derisively.

Research has shown that rigidly hierarchical business environments and senior managers with most status to lose exhibit the greatest resistance to having their beliefs challenged.

How to Avoid This Trap

Constantly put your most cherished assumptions and beliefs on trial. Become a prosecuting attorney rather than always speaking for the defence. Seek out fresh evidence that may disprove your convictions instead of paying attention only to facts in support of those views.

Always keep in mind that 'innovative thinking' does not mean seeing what nobody has ever seen before, but seeing what everybody has seen, but in a new light. It is this ability to notice things that others have ignored or dismissed that has led to many of the world's greatest and most valuable discoveries.

MIND TRAP EIGHT: THE CHALLENGE OF CHANGE

Because Unconscious Knowledge can be used so easily and effortlessly, it may blind us to the fact that new information or changes in external circumstances have completely altered the workplace situation. This can result in serious errors and misjudgements.

This trap is very likely to arise at times of rapid change, during what have been termed 'paradigm shifts' in which the old order is overturned and new rules apply.

How to Avoid This Trap

Always be on the lookout for new ideas, insights, facts and figures. Become an avid collector of information about as wide a range of subjects as possible. Use the Skim and Scan reading techniques described in the next chapter, not just to keep up with the latest developments in your own field but to stimulate your brain and keep your thinking fresh.

Keep on learning throughout your entire career. Memory improves with practice, so the more you use the less you lose. Use the 'Learning Machine' described in Chapter Five to acquire new knowledge quickly and with a minimum of effort.

Having acquired fresh knowledge, be sure to use it regularly. As the learning ladder shows, it is possible to slip from Unconscious Knowledge to Unconscious Ignorance through neglecting an activity to the point where it is forgotten.

MIND TRAP NINE: NOT KNOWING WHAT YOU KNOW

Hewlett-Packard's CEO Lew Platt, once commented that: 'If HP knew what HP knows, we would be three times as profitable!'[8] The difficulty arises largely because the exponential growth in our ability to store, retrieve and communicate information has greatly outpaced our ability to keep track of it all. We know that the 'truth is out there somewhere', but all too often, try as we may, it remains elusive. Anyone who has tried to search for information on the Internet will know just how stressful and frustrating a task this can be. As Arthur C. Clarke has said, finding information from the Net can be like trying to drink from Niagara Falls.

How to Avoid This Trap

Constantly review your knowledge base, using the latest software to help you keep track of data. If your business involves searching either the Internet or Intranets for new information, make sure that the techniques used are those best suited to the challenge. On the Internet, information hunting can be performed using one of two systems, either directories or search engines.

Directories are compiled by people who have visited the pages, whereas search engines have been automatically compiled by software that scours the World Wide Web. Directories catalogue fewer pages than search engines, but they are able to provide short reviews and give some indication of the quality of the page.

Search engines (see the box below) list a far greater number of sites because they are automated and continuously prowl the Internet and make a note of everything they find.

Search engines are organized into three systems. The **robot** (or **spider**) moves around on the Internet looking for new pages. It can take days or weeks for a robot to search the whole of the World Wide Web. When the robot has found a new page, it is placed into the **index**, which has a particular method of organizing the pages. One can then search for a page on a subject by searching the index via a **query module**.

Metasearch engines work by searching through several search engines. However, they are slower and cannot offer as many features as real search engines.

Each search engine has its own idiosyncrasies, its own methods of organizing information and accessing it. Therefore, it is worthwhile using more than one search engine whenever you are searching for something important.

CHOOSING THE RIGHT SEARCH ENGINE

www.hotbot.com
The index has more than 53 million Web pages. This is probably the best engine currently available. It is fast and allows many refinements in your search (searches can be narrowed according to time, location and how closely the site matches your search description).

www.lycos.com
Lycos, half search engine and half directory, covers about 100 million pages. It gives a top 5 per cent of Web pages as rated by reviewers. However, it does not have the advanced search features of hotbot.

Altavista.digital.com
Enables the user to conduct advanced searches (including foreign languages) of over 30 million pages. It is one of the fastest search engines.

www.infoseek.com
Infoseek is a search engine with an index of about 50 million pages. There are four versions of this engine: Ultrasmart (the most basic), Ultraseek (with more advanced search capabilities), Newscenter (news headlines) and Smartinfo (enables searches for basic information such as e-mail addresses, phone numbers and stock quotations).

www.excite.com
Like lycos, excite is half search engine and half directory. The search engine has more than 50 million pages indexed, while the directory has over 150,000 reviewed sites. Excite has medium capability to conduct searches and the ability to find information on the news,

weather, e-mail addresses and stock information. Also, excite gives Web-based e-mail to anyone who uses it.

www.metacrawler.com
This metasearch engine sends inquiries to excite, altavista, lycos, infoseek, WebCrawler and Yahoo! No advanced search features, although you can narrow searches by location and word/phrase.

Improved search engines are being developed all the time. One of the best at the moment is Autonomy, which uses a complex mathematical model to track down elusive information on the Web's more than 30 million pages. This technology automatically categorizes, hyperlinks, cross-references and creates personal information for individual users. It does this by first identifying the employee's levels of expertise by creating a profile based on the content of previous searches as well as ideas in the documents and e-mails he or she exchanges.

SUMMARY

In this chapter I have described nine traps that can lead to errors and misjudgements. Although overload is not directly responsible for all these traps, in every case working with large amounts of information, especially under the pressure of deadlines, does make them more likely to arise but less likely to be noticed. Reduce this risk by:

- taking more time to reflect on new information and to review it more objectively
- finding the fastest and most efficient ways of tracking down relevant information
- never being dazzled by something new just because of its novelty.

3 Beyond Rapid Reading

'Print on paper is a little like democracy: the worst possible system except for all the others. Books are fragile, they are bulky, they are not easy to search through ... Yet printed volumes have endured half a millennium as readable as the day they came off the press, whereas digital data a mere thirty years old may have vanished past hope of retrieval.'

Paul Wallich, *Preserving the Word*[1]

We are what we read.

Around 70 per cent of everything we know comes via the written word, which suggests that much of our success in life depends on being able to read rapidly, easily and efficiently. Unfortunately, the reading skills of even intelligent and well-educated people are usually deficient. Studies suggest that many of us read at 250 words per minute or less, not much quicker than normal talking speed.

You can check your current reading speed by following the procedure in the box below.

ASSESSING YOUR READING SPEED

Set yourself realistic goals for increasing your reading speed by first establishing your present rate. To do this:

- Choose some unfamiliar material that is similar to texts you normally or frequently read in the course of your work.
- Using a watch, read for exactly one minute. When doing so, bear in mind that you must understand the text to an extent that

matches your reading purpose. This is the key to efficient reading and one that I will describe in detail below. There is no point in racing through the text if the understanding obtained would be inadequate to satisfy your workplace needs.

- Calculate the number of words read as follows. Total the number of words in ten lines. Now divide the total by 10 to obtain the average number of words per line.
- Count how many lines you read in one minute and multiply by the average number of words per line to obtain a figure for your current reading speed.

For example:
- Number of lines read in 60 seconds = 60
- Number of words in ten lines = 91
- Average number of words per line = 91 ÷ 10 = 9
- Reading speed = 60 × 9 = 540 words per minute.

Such a speed would be well above the normal average, but it is still far short of what can be attained with the right technique and a little practice.

There are, of course, exceptions to this slow average reading speed. Some people develop ways of reading extremely rapidly with excellent comprehension. President John F. Kennedy for example was able to read between 1,000 and 3,000 words a minute, Teddy Roosevelt averaged three books a day while in the White House, and philosopher John Stuart Mill grumbled that he could never turn the pages fast enough.

To understand how this gulf between potential and normally achieved reading speeds comes about, we need to look at the way most children learn to read in the first place.

HOW WE LEARN TO READ

Not long ago, I was sitting opposite a man in the train who was reading an upmarket newspaper that claims to be read by 'top people'. Certainly, from the way he was dressed, I assumed this middle-aged, grey-haired, distinguished-looking individual held a senior position in some company or other. What struck me about him was the way he was reading his paper. As his gaze moved slowly and methodically across the page, I could see his lips silently mouthing the words his eyes were taking in. He was reading 'aloud' inside his head.

That man is far from unusual. Even when there are no lip movements to betray the fact, many people first translate printed symbols into silent sounds and then make sense of this voice inside their head. This entirely unnecessary step merely slows down the acquisition of new knowledge, since written texts can be interpreted directly. Indeed, we do this every day with well-known words and phrases. When you see a STOP or SLOW sign when driving, the meaning is immediately apparent without having to 'voice' the words.

Adults who read inefficiently are not to blame, since that's the way most of us were taught. Think back to your earliest reading lessons; they probably involved standing up in class, holding the book open in trembling hands and reading aloud a passage selected by the teacher. If you missed a word, you were sent back to read the sentence again.

As a result, two powerfully unhelpful habits were instilled into your brain at the very start of your education. The first was to turn symbols on the page into sounds in your head. The second was a reluctance, amounting almost to guilt in some readers, to skip a single word.

Such habits are neither necessary nor desirable. The written word can be interpreted reliably and accurately without the symbol-to-sound stage, and the degree of redundancy in virtually all texts permits a considerable amount of skipping without loss of comprehension.

Reading, like thinking (of which it is a crucial part), is a dynamic process to which each of us brings a lifetime of experience, thoughts, feelings, observations, actions and knowledge, everything, in fact, that helps to make us a unique human being. Because reading is an aspect of thinking, rather than an exercise in eye movement, speed alone is not the key issue. Woody Allen once quipped that he had taken a speed reading course and finished *War and Peace* in four minutes. 'It's about Russia!' he said.

What matters is your level of understanding, which, in turn, depends on your reading purpose. Provided this purpose is achieved, you can read as rapidly as you wish and skip as much of the material as you like.

DECIDING WHAT'S WORTH READING

Fully understanding your reading *purpose* is the first essential step to saving yourself time and fatigue when confronted by the volumes of texts with which information workers must routinely deal. Before doing any more than glancing briefly through any text, ask yourself the following questions.

Why am I reading this? What personal or professional goals will the knowledge it provides help me achieve?

If you are able to answer this question satisfactorily, then ask yourself: is this text the most suitable one for achieving my reading purpose?

Sometimes you can answer these questions without doing more than glancing through the text; on other occasions a somewhat closer examination – which still stops far short of reading the entire contents – may be needed.

While this may seem like no more than simple common sense, my experience has been that much time and effort are wasted by trying to gather information which is either unnecessary or which could be obtained more easily from a different text.

Once you have a clear idea of your reading purpose, the next step is to consider how useful the text in question is likely to prove in satisfying this goal.

CALCULATING THE USEFULNESS INDEX

There is a simple formula that provides clear guidance as to the value of any given text, by allowing you to calculate its rating on a 'Usefulness Index'. Developed by three doctors, this Index has been successfully used to evaluate a variety of the sources used by the medical profession.

$$\text{Usefulness Index} = \frac{\text{Relevance} \times \text{Validity}}{\text{Work Required to Access}}$$

As the creators of this formula, Doctors Allen Shaughnessy, David Slawson and Joshua Bennett point out: 'The goal of information mastery is to determine the information source with the highest usefulness score.

Working too hard to establish validity raises the work and decreases the overall usefulness of the information. On the other hand, a low work source may also have low validity, relevance or both. The best source of information provides highly relevant and valid information and can be obtained with minimal effort.'[2]

To obtain a Usefulness Index for any text, you must first make three judgements:

1. How relevant is the information to my present needs? This is largely determined by how often you are presented with the particular problem being addressed.
2. How valid is the information? This depends on a wide range of factors, including the source of the material, how recent it is, the authority of the author or authors, and any possible sources of bias.

One Fleet Street editor remembers how, as a young journalist, he was advised by his editor that when interviewing politicians he should constantly ask himself: 'Why is this lying bastard lying to me?'

Given the amount of misinformation, disinformation, propaganda and downright lies currently in circulation, such a sceptical approach is no less prudent today. It is often risky to accept any evidence at face value simply because it has been published in a prestigious book or journal. If you lack the expertise to make a valid judgement, it is a time-saving rather than a time-wasting strategy to seek out somebody expert in that field.

3. How much time and effort will it take to find the information I require?

One way of approaching the task of assessing the value of a text is to rate each of the three factors on a scale of 1 to 10, where 1 indicates the lowest possible evaluation and 10 the highest.

Taking the first judgement, that of **relevance**:

> 1 = Low: little or no relevance
> 5 = Medium: moderately relevant
> 10 = High: entirely relevant

The second judgement, **validity**, would similarly be rated as:

1 = Low: little or no validity
5 = Medium: some valid/some invalid information
10 = High: entirely valid

For the third and final judgement, estimate how much **work** and effort you will need to put into understanding the information.

1 = Low: easily accessed
5 = Medium: moderately easy to access
10 = High: requires considerable work to access

Clearly this judgement depends on a number of variables, such as your own knowledge and experience, together with why an author has communicated his or her ideas. Used in this way, the Usefulness Index will provide a final figure between 0.1 (little relevance or value, and almost impossible to read) and 100 (extremely relevant and valid, useful, extremely easy to read).

For example: Article in tabloid newspaper:

Relevance = 1
Validity = 2
Work = 1
Usefulness = $2 \times 1 \div 1 = 2$ almost entirely useless

Technical journal from one's own area of expertise:

Relevance = 8
Validity = 9
Work = 5
Usefulness = $8 \times 9 \div 5 = 14$

Technical journal outside one's own area of expertise:

Relevance = 7
Validity = 8
Work = 9
Usefulness = $7 \times 8 \div 9 = 6$

Ratings in the table below were obtained by asking information workers in a number of fields to assess a range of publications and then taking an average and rounding off to a single digit.

Usefulness of Frequently Used Information Sources

Information Source	Relevance	Validity	Work	Rating
Regularly updated manual	8	9	7	10
Internet in 10 years' time	9	9	4	20
Colleagues	8	6	3	16
Tabloid press	2	2	1	4
Broadsheet press	5	6	3	10
Technical press	8	8	5	13
Internet now	4	3	9	1

CONDUCT A SIXTY-SECOND SURVEY

To judge the relevance, validity and amount of work needed to understand the printed text, you should start by conducting a rapid survey of the material. This should take no more than a minute to complete.

One: Relevance

Spend twenty seconds glancing at the title, sub-title, jacket blurb (if a book), abstract or summary (if a paper). Identify the source of the material. Look at the date of the publication. While doing so, keep these questions in mind:

● What, if anything, do I know about the author and publisher?
● Is the information current or likely to be dated?
● What do I already know about this topic?
● How will reading this help me?
● From what I have seen so far, does the text appear *relevant* to my current needs?

If the answer to the last question is no, then the other two factors of *validity* and *work* can be safely ignored. If, however, the answer is either 'yes' or 'possibly', you can rate relevance on a scale of 1 (almost no relevance at all) to 10 (highly relevant) as described above and move to the next stage, which should also take no more than twenty seconds.

Two: Validity

Skim read any preface or foreword to discover whether this helps you understand the author's purpose and theme. This may also provide an insight into the probable complexity of the text. Flick through the material, glancing at any charts, maps, diagrams, chapter headings, cross-references within chapters and illustrations. Notice which key points emerge from this general overview.

Now ask yourself:

● How reliable is the source (i.e. author, publisher, journal)?
● Is there likely to be any bias which would make the information suspect?
● Does the author have a vested interest in persuading me to accept this information as valid?
● If a book, has it been endorsed by other experts in the field?
● If a technical paper, does the author come from a reputable company, institution or organization?

Rate the validity on the scale of 1 (very likely to be invalid) to 10 (entirely accurate and reliable) as described above.

Three: Work Needed to Access Information

In the final twenty seconds, skim read the first and last two paragraphs of the text to gain an impression as to the complexity of the material. Ask yourself:

● Is this text intended for readers with far greater knowledge of the subject than I possess?
● If so, can I still find and understand what I need in order to serve my reading purpose without devoting excessive amounts of time and energy to the text?
● Even if the subject is reasonably familiar to me, is the writer's approach and style such that he/she communicates clearly and unambiguously?

Rate this final factor on a scale of 10 (high degree of work needed) to 1 (little or no work) as before.

Calculate the Usefulness Index for that material and make a note of it. This will save you having to reassess the text should you return to it at some time in the future. Where a number of alternative sources for the information exist, you will be able to go directly to the most useful texts.

Having completed your survey, set the material aside and spend a moment or two reflecting on the information. How certain are you that it will truly satisfy your reading purpose?

By having a basic grasp of the text, the ideas it contains may spring to mind while you are working on a completely different topic. The power of serendipity, the chance discovery, cannot be underestimated. At the end of each day, I will usually select a book, paper or report at random from the library and carry out a sixty-second survey on the text. While doing so, my purpose is to expand my general knowledge of that particular subject. Weeks – maybe months – later, while writing or researching a project, the idea I picked up from that material may suddenly spring into my mind.

DEVELOPING FLAIR

One problem with some of the rapid reading courses and training programmes on the market is that they require you to make fundamental changes in the way you read.

While this may yield excellent results in the long term, changing any well-established pattern of behaviour – especially a skill which has been as over-learnt as reading – is time-consuming and tedious.

As you struggle to master the new procedures, you will probably suffer a sharp fall in your normal reading speed. Given the pressures most information workers are currently under, to me this seems unacceptable.

Rather than taking the time needed to master a new way of reading, it is more sensible, and much less stressful, simply to modify your present approach to reading. The programme I have developed in my course is called FLAIR. This stands for **FL**exible **A**nd **I**nteractive **R**eading.

I have found it not only the most efficient way of dealing with texts of all kinds, but also the easiest by far to master. Unlike some 'rapid reading' techniques, FLAIR can be put to work straight away with little or no alteration of reading habits.

FLAIR involves reading in an active rather than a passive manner, by moving very rapidly through some parts of the text, while slowing on key sections and interacting with the text, in the manner described by American author William Safir: '. . . read sceptically, often doubtfully, sometimes combatively, inwardly commenting "Good" or "Wrong" or "Why?" and lubricating or challenging the prose by mentally larding in personal experience in support or refutation.'[3]

This approach incorporates the two fundamental principles found in all effective reading programmes: the crucial need to make reading an active and conscious process rather than a passive one, and the importance of reading everything. In the highly competitive world of modern business you dare not automatically assume that anything is 'junk'. Ideas and inspirations can be found in the most unlikely sources. Until a text is assigned a Usefulness Index, which can be done only by rapidly reading it, no piece of writing should be dismissed as valueless.

FLAIR IN ACTION

Imagine you are prospecting for minerals on a newly discovered desert island. One method would be simply to land on the nearest beach and set off in a direction chosen at random, noting down all the interesting features found along the way. Having reached the other side of the island, you then repeat the process, criss-crossing the island until every square yard has been charted. Clearly such an approach is not only extremely time-consuming but it is likely to provide you with far more information than you actually need to achieve your purpose.

Described in these terms, such a slow, methodical and effortful strategy seems absurd. Yet this is the way the majority set about reading. They start at the first page and continue zigzagging backwards and forwards through the lines of text until eventually they reach the last.

An alternative, and far more efficient, way of prospecting would be to fly over the island at sufficient height to gain a good overview of the whole place, so identifying the areas of greatest significance. You could then retrace your course over just those areas, this time flying much lower so that more details were apparent. Having done this, you would abandon your flying machine and set out on foot to examine thoroughly the areas of interest. Efficient reading involves adopting a similar strategy.

Start by taking a general view of the text; this is the equivalent of your first, high-altitude flight over the island. Because you have already become familiar with the material during your sixty-second survey, the first sweep can be fairly rapid.

At this point, pause for a moment and consider whether you need to continue reading the material. Now that you have a clearer idea of what this particular 'island' has to offer, are you certain it can satisfy your reading purpose? If not, it makes sense to find another 'island' more likely to reward the time spent in exploration.

Assuming you decide to read on, your next step is to rearrange the text so that it best suits your reading purpose. You might decide, for example, that Chapters 1, 4 and 12 would provide you with all the information necessary to satisfy your reading purpose. These can then be explored in depth, using a combination of the three methods for reading that will be described below.

The final stage is to label the sections, paragraphs, sentences or words of greatest relevance by underlining or highlighting them, adding notes and comments in the margin. By interacting with text in this way you will not only develop a far more thorough understanding of the material but will significantly improve your ability to remember key facts and figures.

BE FLEXIBLE – CHANGE MENTAL GEAR AS YOU READ

Vary your reading speed according to the type of material being read and your reading purpose. There are three reading speeds:

High gear – Skimming. Rapid but somewhat superficial. An excellent way of getting an overall grasp of what the text is all about and discovering which sections of text will need to be Scanned.

Medium gear – Scanning. Slower. Get a more in-depth understanding and identify those sections that will need to be read with care by means of . . .

Low gear – Studying. The slowest of all. Provides a comprehensive understanding of crucial elements of the text.

Skimming

This is the fastest way of reading, with speeds of 1,000-plus words per minute easily achievable. Its purpose is to move rapidly through the material while searching for a general idea or a few specific points. The answers to questions sought through skimming are usually clearly presented in the text and do not need seeking out. They also tend to be fairly short, maybe no more than two or three words. When skimming, read the material swiftly and lightly. Do not try to read each and every word, but let your eyes run down the page rather than moving from left to right across the lines, until one of the key facts is located.

The best way of training your eye to move down the page, absorbing information, is by moving your hand or a card down the page. This was the basic secret of rapid reading discovered by Evelyn Wood, and it came about purely by chance.

Although she was a specialist in reading, and her course had been adopted by teachers all over the USA, Evelyn herself was unable to improve her own reading speed, something that caused her great annoyance. One day, while reading a book called *Green Mansions* in a field outside the cabin she and her husband owned, Evelyn became so frustrated by her slow reading speed that she flung the book away. When she tried to read it again, later that night, there was mud on the page. Brushing it away caused her to stumble upon the key to rapid reading: her hand gave her eye something to follow down the page, thus vastly increasing her reading speed. Using this simple technique she finished *Green Mansions* in ten minutes!

This works because our vision has evolved to pay attention to anything that moves. Recall the experiment I described in Chapter One, in which your fingers, stretched out on either side of your head at the periphery of vision, become invisible until you wiggle them. When something moves, our eyes follow it. I shall describe how to pace your reading using a hand or card later in this chapter.

As you skim the text, seek out answers to the questions: Who? What? When? and Where? Who was involved? What happened? When did it happen? Where did it happen?

By holding one or more of these questions uppermost in your mind as you skim through the text, you will find the required answers jump right off the page at you.

Skimming is the fastest form of reading, but it will allow you only to answer questions requiring literal or factual answers.

Scanning

As with skimming-type questions, scan questions are frequently factual or literal and are mainly useful in organizing material. The answers may be more difficult to locate and may demand more effort, because they often require a careful ordering of ideas.

Scanning involves moving at a slightly slower pace through the text, achieving speeds of between 500 and 1,000 words per minute. Scanning enables you to search for answers to longer and more complex questions, starting with Why? and How? Why did some event happen? How did it happen?

Suppose, for instance, you are seeking information about different applications for a new industrial product. You scan the text searching for the word 'application' or words and phrases with a similar meaning. This guides you to an orderly selection of the sections which contain information relating to your reading purpose. Provided you *really* know what you are looking for, you will find the required facts and figures almost seem to jump off the page and demand your attention.

Studying

Finally there is critical reading, where the material is explored in detail for deeper meanings. But, just as only a small area of the island needed to be surveyed on foot, so too is there only a limited amount of text that demands this most detailed form of reading.

Studying involves making judgements, reading reflectively, and reading to absorb new and unfamiliar ideas. The questions you pose while studying demand more than literal information to answer them. You must often read between the lines and apply your critical faculties to the statements made. Study reading is the slowest process of all because it requires you to pause and reflect on what has just been read.

By starting with a well-established purpose, however, your thinking will be directed so clearly that even study reading can be accomplished far more rapidly than in the past.

USE A PACER CARD FOR SKIMMING OR SCANNING

Some people find they can skim or scan more easily and effectively by guiding their eyes down the page using a sheet of plain card (or their hand) as a pacer. If you would like to experiment with this technique, here's how you set about it.

1. Place the card, or your hand, flat on the page *above* the printed line. By covering what has just been read, you can prevent time wasted through unnecessary backtracking.
2. Move the card (or your hand) quickly down the page, keeping your gaze fixed on the line directly beneath it.
3. Adjust your reading speed by making the card, or hand, move slower or faster down the page according to the material. Make certain your eyes keep pace with the guide.
4. Do not try to read an entire line at once. Instead, identify whatever words you can in each line as the card/hand pushes your eyes down the page.
5. At the start, move your pacer hand or card only slightly faster than your normal reading speed. Increase speed as confidence develops through practice. This will ensure you remain relaxed while gradually raising the rate at which you take in text.

HOW YOU CAN READ ROUTINE TEXTS MORE RAPIDLY

By knowing where to look for the information you require with six common types of business reading, you will save time by directing your gaze straight to the right spot on the page.

1. *Newspapers and Magazines*

These contain three types of material: feature articles, opinion articles and news stories.

FEATURE ARTICLES

Their purpose is to inform and entertain. They provide background material on the topic and typically illustrate key ideas with examples and anecdotes. They normally start with an example of what the writer has in mind.

How To Read Feature Articles Rapidly

Scan the material, directing your attention mainly to the middle and final portions of the text, since this typically contains the key ideas and facts. You can usually skip the first and last paragraphs without any loss of comprehension, since these contain illustrative anecdotes and examples.

OPINION ARTICLES

These are intended to direct your thinking over a particular issue and/or take some action desired by the writer.

How To Read Opinion Articles Rapidly

Frequently you will need to read only the first two or three paragraphs which typically contain the main ideas or actions being advocated and the final paragraph which summarizes the key points. The paragraphs between usually offer reasons and examples in support of the opinion offered. These may not be necessary for you to understand the argument and may safely be ignored.

NEWS STORIES

Unlike feature articles, these usually contain mostly facts with few if any examples or anecdotes and little or no background material.

How To Read News Stories Rapidly

- Most prioritize information, starting with what the editor or journalist considers the most significant facts and ending with the information regarded as of least importance.
- Read the first and last paragraphs before skimming the intervening material.
- In a news magazine, diagrams, charts and graphs may be used to summarize the main ideas, statistics and concepts. Examine these first to gain an overview of the content.
- With magazines, always begin by going through the table of contents to identify articles relevant to your reading purpose.
- When reading for work rather than pleasure, never spend time browsing and resist being distracted by interesting but irrelevant articles.

Clip relevant but non-urgent articles and keep them in your briefcase or desk so they can be read during otherwise 'dead times', such as waiting for an appointment or when travelling by plane or train.

If you collect a great many cuttings, organize them into files. You might, for example, have one for articles about competitors, another for technology, a third for marketing features, and so forth. By gathering material on the same topic from various sources, you get a more rounded view of the subject. It also becomes easier to assess the validity of any one article by comparing it with other views and opinions.

2. Reading Memos More Rapidly

Study your company memos and you'll probably find they have a similar structure, with key information, e.g. source, subject and intent (information or action requested), located in the same place on each occasion.

Save time by going directly to these target areas. There is rarely any need to read the entire memo. If especially busy and faced by a stack of memos, use skim reading to sort those with a high priority to your right and those with a lower priority to your left. That way you can work rapidly through those demanding immediate attention or action, while leaving the others for a spare moment.

3. Reading Company Reports More Rapidly

- Skim read in order to obtain an overview and gain a general idea both of the individual components of the report and how they have been organized.
- Even if a table of contents is provided, it is still worthwhile scanning the report in order to locate any sub-headings left off the contents list.
- Recheck your reading purpose. What will you want or need to do with the information contained in the report?
- On a sheet of scrap paper scribble down a contents list of your own. Note the page numbers of key ideas, facts, diagrams, graphs, etc.
- Rank this in order of your personal priority. This could well be different from the printed contents list, which reflects the author's priorities.
- Finally, skim, scan or study relevant sections, always keeping your reading purpose firmly in mind.

4. Reading Technical Material More Rapidly

These texts are among the mentally most demanding you ever have to read, for several reasons:

1. Concepts and ideas are usually complex and demand careful thought.
2. Specialized terms and phrases may require precise interpretation.
3. The style is often dense and the material poorly organized.
4. Print size may be small and sentences mind-numbingly lengthy.
5. Diagrams, illustrations, charts and formulae are often poorly located in relation to relevant text.
6. Background knowledge underlying the often complex procedures or concepts is usually assumed by the authors and is not included in the text.

How To Read Them

As always, start by defining your reading purpose. Ask yourself:

- What do I need/want to get out of this text?
- What depth of understanding will be necessary to achieve that purpose?
- Is this book/report the best way of satisfying my reading purpose?

● Is it intended for a reader with my level of knowledge?
● What authority does the author bring to the report? Is he or she a recognized authority in this particular area? Are the writer's credentials sufficiently impressive to make my investment of time worthwhile?
● How recent is the material? Bear in mind that, in many fast-developing fields, a report may be, to a greater or lesser extent, out of date almost as soon as it has been published. In other words, what is its validity rating?
● Calculate the Usefulness Index and, if there are a number of different possible sources for the information needed, always go to the one with the highest index.

If you decide a report or manual will have to be read, proceed as follows:

STEP ONE: Review the material and get an idea of its overall structure. Ask yourself:

● Are there charts, illustrations, etc., that will help you understand key concepts and ideas?
● How complex is the material? How much work will be required to make sense of the information it contains?
● Does it include descriptions, procedures, case histories, problems and ways of solving them?
● Are key concepts explained or is an understanding of them assumed?
● What help is provided for the reader? Is there, for instance, a glossary of technical terms and acronyms?
● Is there a table of contents and, if so, is this detailed or superficial? If it is superficial, you may find it helpful to create your own table of contents.

Identify those concepts, words and phrases which best communicate the author's key ideas. If you are unfamiliar with any of them, be sure to clarify your understanding of each one before reading on. Such ideas can usually be found in three specific areas of the text:
(i) Table of contents – especially when this is detailed. Never skip the contents table, since this often provides an indispensable overview of how ideas have been organized.
(ii) Introduction or preface. Many readers skip them in the mistaken belief that this will save time. Since many writers describe the major

purpose of their book or the chief premise of the report here, the introduction or preface should always be read. In addition they often summarize the text and may also explain key concepts.

(iii) First and last paragraphs in chapters or report sections.

Dip in and out of the text, making no attempt to speed read any of the material at this stage. Having done so, put the book or report down and think about the information you have gained so far. Jot down any questions which the material raises in your mind.

Now ask yourself once again: do I need to read this after all?

If your answer is still 'Yes', start by reading the section or chapter most relevant to your needs. Do not assume you have to begin at the beginning and work through in sequence to the end. Simply because that structure suited the writer's purpose does not mean it will also suit your own. Where necessary, re-prioritize the material and read it in that order.

Identify those sections of the text that are most likely to give you the greatest difficulty and develop a strategy for dealing with them.

If there are unfamiliar technical terms, acronyms, company codes, definitions and so on, note these down – together with an explanation – on a separate sheet of paper.

STEP TWO: Identify your reading purpose.

With the preliminary survey completed, the next stage is to consider how this material will help you achieve your reading purpose. You will also have a better idea of what parts of the text, such as terminology or assumptions about your prior knowledge, are likely to cause trouble.

Skim or scan each section to obtain an overview, then focus on key paragraphs and study them more thoroughly.

Read the relevant parts actively by labelling key ideas, concepts and information in the text. If you are unable to write on the book or report itself, then photocopy appropriate pages. Underline any parts that require further study. Highlight key words and concepts in each paragraph.

STEP THREE: Read interactively.

- Read a section of text first to gain an overview – as when flying across the island in the example above – before reading it in greater detail.
- Constantly changing your focus aids your understanding and recall for absorbing the information by keeping your mind alert and directed. You may find it helpful to re-edit particularly complicated sections, reducing their length and eliminating redundancies.

• Carve lengthy sections into manageable blocks of text and set yourself the goal of reading one or two of these at a time. This prevents boredom and makes it far easier to stay focused. With especially complex texts in which a high level of understanding is necessary, clarify the content by condensing it. Underline key words and phrases so that the main points in the material stand out.

READING YOUR MAIL MORE RAPIDLY

In the course of a lifetime, people in business can expect to receive at least 50,000 items of unsolicited direct mail, also known as 'junk mail'. Assuming it takes a minute to open and glance through each one of these, you will end up spending some five months of your life solely engaged in this largely unproductive chore.

Yet tossing these, unopened, into the waste bin, as many people do, could mean missing out on an idea of great importance to you. Instead, use rapid reading to decide within a few seconds whether or not a document is useful, so reducing your lifetime investment down to just a few days.

Open letters over a waste-paper basket. That way you can drop any unwanted items straight into the bin after quickly evaluating them.

Handle each item once only. Decide immediately what action to take, even if it is to place the letter in a file to be dealt with later. Grouping similar tasks in this way improves productivity by aiding focus and concentration.

If interested, respond by phone, fax or e-mail to save time. Alternatively, make a brief comment on the original letter or on an attached sticky Post-it note and then fax or mail back.

FIVE RULES FOR FATIGUE-FREE READING

1. Eliminate all movements of the lips, head and hands when reading. These slow you down and distract you from what is being read.
2. Stay as physically relaxed and comfortable as possible. If possible, read while sitting in an easy chair.

3. Try to read phrases, sentences and even paragraphs, rather than single words.
4. Try not to let your mind wander. If you find yourself thinking of something else, write a note about it and take it up later.
5. Try to anticipate the argument the author is setting out. Ask yourself whether he or she is developing his or her ideas on the lines you would expect.

SAVING TIME WHEN WRITING

Before leaving the topic of reading written texts, it's worth considering the following practical ways in which you, as the author of a document, can help colleagues and subordinates save time and fatigue when reading them.

1 Know What It Is You Want To Say

Start by establishing clearly, in your own mind, why you are writing the text. What is your writing purpose?

What is the level of knowledge, experience and interest of those who will be expected to read your communication? This identifies the scope of your writing and enables you to bring the topic into focus more clearly. Is the text intended to inform or to persuade? Is it a combination of both?

With the answer to this question in mind, write a basic structure for your document. This allows you to identify the key points with which you will develop your message. These points should always be organized in a logical, consistent and meaningful way. For example:

> Prevention – Cure
> Problem – Solution
> Cause – Effect

2 Prepare an Outline

An outline helps you think clearly about your ideas and keeps you on track while writing.

A helpful exercise is to summarize the main points in no more than fifty words. This is the number of words that can be read easily and comfortably in less than thirty seconds.

Start with an introduction. This should clearly describe your aims and the areas to be covered.

Next produce a point-by-point summary of your proposed message.

Finally, draw your conclusion(s). This/these should be clear and convincing. One way of doing this is to write down a series of headings, each with its set of related bullet points. This lets you see at a glance the overall structure and warns you should you begin to go off at a tangent.

If there are a large number of bullet points under a particular heading, this may mean that you are entering into unnecessary detail. Try breaking down that single heading into two or more items.

3 Getting Started

For most writers, the hardest part is getting started. Here are six proven ways to get going:

1. On a first draft do not worry about getting the content 100 per cent correct. Write down your ideas as rapidly as possible, even if this leads to poorly constructed sentences. It is easier to edit existing material than to write it down perfectly in the first place.
2. Maintaining a rapid writing pace will ensure your creative juices keep flowing.
3. Never stop to re-read what you have just written when preparing the first draft or you may lose the thread of your ideas. If you have difficulty knowing where to begin, just write down any thoughts related to your presentation which come to mind. While writing, vary your sentence length and avoid too-lengthy ones. As a general rule, the shorter the sentence, the better.
4. If you get badly stuck, try speaking your ideas aloud into a tape or dictation machine. Putting ideas into words often breaks down any blocks to creativity.
5. While it is important to use technical expressions where relevant, avoid any suggestion of jargon. Ruthlessly excise all words that make your message sound pompous, ponderous, patronizing or pedantic.
6. The parts of any text we read first and last remain most clearly in our memory. This is called the 'primacy' and 'recency' effect. Be sure to

outline your key facts, figures, ideas and arguments at the start, then summarize them again at the end.

Keep in mind that, no matter what your topic or how long the message, a logical structure is essential to aid your readers' understanding. They must be helped to follow your arguments as rapidly and as easily as the nature of the material allows.

7. Keep in mind KISS – 'Keep It Straightforward and Simple'. If you can say something in 100 words, why waste everybody's time by using 1,000? As an American congressman grumbled recently: 'The Lord's Prayer, the Twenty-third Psalm, the United States Declaration of Independence only require a few words. But the United States Department of Agriculture directive on the pricing of a cabbage has 15,629 words. You do have to ask: "Hey guys, what the heck are we doing?" If you can write these fundamental laws of mankind of how we're going to live, and then a major prayer to the deity, and the basis on which a nation will operate, do we really need all these words to buy a cabbage?'

SUMMARY

I've covered a lot of ground in this chapter, so let's just summarize the key procedures you should adopt from now on in order to combat this important aspect of information overload.

Essentially there are just six steps to follow, and you should practise and repeat these until they achieve the level of Unconscious Knowledge discussed in Chapter Two. Once that level of proficiency has been achieved, you will find it possible to dramatically reduce the time spent accessing written information, as well as obtaining much greater insight into the material under review. What is more, because you have prepared your mind to take on board the new information, learning and comprehension will also prove far easier. In the words of philosopher Jean-Jacques Rousseau: 'Minds well prepared are the monuments where knowledge is most surely engraved.'

1. Start by deciding whether or not to read a text. Will knowing the information it contains help you to achieve extra or enhanced personal and/or professional goals?
2. Calculate the Usefulness Index by assigning number values to the

relevance, validity and ease of access of the material. Multiply relevance by usefulness and then divide by ease of access. If you have a number of texts on a similar subject, assess each of them in this way and then make a start on the material that possess the highest index rating.

3. When you start to read, do so flexibly and interactively by using what I called the FLAIR approach. Never try to absorb the information passively, as a sponge soaks up liquid. The brain functions most efficiently when it is actively involved in the text. Ask questions of the text and track down the answers. Challenge any assumptions or conclusions made by the author. Read sceptically, quizzically and doubtfully.

4. As a reading machine your brain has three gears: high, medium and low. These translate into skimming (very rapid reading), scanning (moderate speed) and study (slow). Never read an entire text at the same rate. Skim to get an overview of the text and identify key passages and ideas. The questions to keep in mind here are: Who? What? When? and Where?

   Use your hand or a card to draw your gaze swiftly down the page.

5. Now scan to search for longer and more complex information, asking and answering questions that begin with Why? and How? Once again, look for the central ideas and supporting evidence.

   Finally slow the pace right down and carefully study those portions of the text of greatest relevance to your needs.

6. By developing an understanding of those texts which form a regular part of your reading, be they magazine articles, technical reports or technical material, you will be able to direct your attention straight to the key content without first having to plough through anything that is less relevant to your reading needs. Like an experienced gold prospector, you will be able to detect the mother lode instantly without wasting any time on the surrounding shale.

4 The Secrets of Successful Learning

'Everything from talking to dying must be learnt.'

Gustave Flaubert, *L'Education sentimentale* (Paris, 1869)

Flaubert's comment expresses a profound, yet seldom recognized, truth about human behaviour. With the exception of a small number of inborn responses, all that we know or believe, strive for or achieve is the result of learning.

'One of the most important effects of the rapid increase in the volume of information is that information is very rapidly rendered obsolete by the discovery of new facts,' commented the late Professor Conrad Waddington[1] as long ago as 1977.

Today, in the words of American futurologist John Naisbitt, we 'mass produce knowledge',[2] and much information has become a highly perishable commodity with an ever shorter use-by date. The only way to stay fresh is through life-long learning. The message from the employment marketplace is brutally direct: keep up the pace or lose your place. Under such circumstances, the ability to learn new information rapidly and efficiently becomes an essential survival skill.

Imagine a student who embarks on a three-year degree course in engineering, graduates at the age of twenty-three with first-class honours, lands a job and starts putting all that hard-learnt knowledge to work.

The company is not interested in employee training so, preoccupied with raising a family, there is little time for our graduate to keep pace with the rapid changes occurring in engineering.

Five years after graduation, what sort of shape is this individual's knowledge likely to be in? The answer depends on the amount of new information and techniques he has accumulated during that half-decade. The American researcher Dr De Solla Price[3] uses the term 'coefficient of immediacy' to describe the growth of knowledge over a specified period.

In this case let us assume that the coefficient of immediacy shows that there has been a 50 per cent increase in new knowledge in the five years since graduation. This implies that, within this period, around half of what was taught no longer applies. In a further five years, if knowledge continues to grow at the same rate, almost everything learnt at university will be so out of date as to be almost valueless.[4] As Professor Waddington puts it: 'The figures are pretty alarming to anyone who thinks all you have to do is learn a certain number of facts at university and they will last you the rest of your life.'

Unfortunately, while information overload is at the root of this problem, it is also one of the main reasons why many people fail to learn efficiently.

HOW OVERLOAD INHIBITS LEARNING

In *Through the Looking-Glass*, the Walrus and the Carpenter are walking along a beach and despairing of ever being able to sweep up all the sand.

> 'If seven maids with seven mops
> Swept it for half a year,
> Do you suppose,' the Walrus said,
> 'That they would get it clear?'
> 'I doubt it,' said the Carpenter,
> And shed a bitter tear.

These days, as they struggle to survive the unending deluge of data, many information workers experience a similar sense of hopelessness. There is just so much out there clamouring to be attended to, analysed, understood and learnt! How can one ever hope to cope?

For many intelligent people, this hopelessness breeds helplessness. A sense of defeat in the face of odds uncounted, an overwhelming belief that, since it is clearly impossible to learn everything there is to be learnt, it's really not worth bothering to learn anything at all.

This denial of reality is often bolstered by an almost magical belief in the power of 'muddling through' and of 'getting by', bolstered by the folk wisdom that 'what you don't know can't hurt you'.

Sadly what you 'don't know' will not just hurt you; it has the potential to destroy you, both professionally and personally.

It is certainly true that, not only can we never know everything about everything, we can't even expect to know everything about anything, as the following calculation makes clear. Each day, around 20 million words of technical information are placed on record. If you were able to read 1,000 words per minute, and you read for eight hours a day without pause, it would take you six weeks just to read through one day's output. At the end of this period you would have fallen behind in your reading by five and a half years![5]

Fortunately, we don't need such a depth of information. What we do need is enough 'working knowledge' to make sensible decisions, solve problems efficiently and creatively, and advance our understanding sufficiently, not just to keep pace with others, but to stay, whenever possible, at least one step ahead of them.

To achieve these reasonable goals, at a time when information is expanding so rapidly, requires a positive outlook, confidence in our ability to learn and superior techniques for mastering facts and figures.

HOW MENTAL FATIGUE INHIBITS LEARNING

The more we work with our brain, the more fatigued it becomes, for reasons that I outlined in Chapter One. To the exhausted mind, even trivial learning tasks can seem impossible. Our mind begins to wander, refusing to stay focused on the task at hand. As neurologist Dr Jeremy M. Wolfe comments: 'If a stimulus is presented while attention is summoned elsewhere, "ere a man hath power to say 'Behold!' The jaws of darkness do devour it up: So quick bright things come to confusion." '[6]

Safeguard yourself against learning fatigue by breaking down each task into study periods of not much more than twenty minutes. That's reckoned to be about the average span of human attention, and flogging away for significantly longer in the hope of drumming a few extra facts and figures into your fatigued brain is a waste of effort. The law of diminishing returns applies here, with less and less being learnt, the longer the continuous period of study.

The traditional image of a student with a wet towel wrapped round his or her weary head, and being kept awake by endless cups of black coffee, is the antithesis of efficient learning.

The best advice is to study the material to be learnt for around twenty minutes, using the interactive methods described below, and then take a break of between five and ten minutes. During this time do not try to recall anything you have just learnt. Set it aside as a period of 'incubation' during which time your brain is able, below the level of awareness, to organize and consolidate what has just been learnt. During your study break, make no attempt at anything intellectually demanding. If possible, go for a stroll, stare out of the window, listen to some music or read an undemanding newspaper or magazine article. While I appreciate that none of these may be possible in a busy office, even in this high-pressure environment you should find some plausible but mentally trivial task with which to occupy yourself until you return to the next twenty-minute period of intensive learning.

After three twenty-minute sessions, take a longer break from the learning task, say of around fifteen minutes. By building your knowledge in this way you will find the learning task is faster, easier, more efficient and far less tiring. If it is possible to do so, do your learning just before going to sleep, since this means that the brain will have seven or eight hours in which to 'incubate' the new information. Never be tempted to study right up to the moment when you switch off the bedside light, however, since you will then find it far harder to drop off. Leave a period of about sixty minutes between finishing your studies and going to sleep. During this mental 'wind-down', listen to music, read an entertaining but undemanding book or watch TV.

In the next chapter I shall be describing some powerful procedures for improving your memory, and these will also help eliminate needless fatigue.

YOUR PERSONAL LEARNING STYLE

The key to learning efficiently, especially under the pressures of information overload, is to match the way new material is organized to your personal learning style.

'When somebody is teaching us in our most comfortable style, we learn,' says American educationalist Bernice McCarthy. 'But more importantly, we feel good about ourselves.'[7]

Discover your own learning style by completing the assessment below.

DISCOVER YOUR PERSONAL LEARNING STYLE

Choose the statement that best describes the way you prefer to study and learn:

1. When studying an unfamiliar subject, I prefer to:
    (a) gather together a variety of information from several sources.
    (b) stick closely to the main theme and master that first of all.

2. I would sooner:
    (a) know a slight amount about a great many subjects.
    (b) become an expert on one or two topics.

3. When studying a book or report, I prefer to:
    (a) skip ahead and read chapters of special interest to me out of sequence.
    (b) start at the beginning and work systematically through to the end.

4. When seeking information from others, I tend to ask questions that require:
    (a) general responses.
    (b) specific answers.

5. When browsing through a library or bookstore, I usually:
    (a) roam around, looking at books on a variety of topics.
    (b) look at books relating to only one or two topics.

6. I am better at remembering:
    (a) broad principles.
    (b) particular facts.

7. When carrying out some task, I like to:
    (a) have background information not strictly related to the job at hand.
    (b) concentrate solely on strictly relevant information.

8. When approaching a new subject, I would rather:
    (a) take an overview of the subject and then fill in details and concepts in my own way.

(b) follow a logical progression of facts from start to finish.

9. If asking for directions to an unfamiliar address, I like to:
   (a) be told clearly how to get there.
   (b) follow a map or diagram.

10. When trying to understand the manual for a new appliance, I usually:
    (a) read the instructions.
    (b) follow the illustrations.

11. When reading a technical report, I look first at:
    (a) the text itself.
    (b) diagrams, flow-charts, graphs and pictures.

12. During a discussion on a topic I am interested in, I am most likely to:
    (a) stand back and listen to what others have to say.
    (b) join in and express my point of view.

13. When listening to a new process being described, I would mainly:
    (a) attend to what was said.
    (b) aid my understanding by creating mental images.

14. When working out a problem, I often:
    (a) jot down relevant words or phrases.
    (b) make doodles and drawings to help picture possible solutions.

15. The phrase I am most likely to use when expressing my understanding of another viewpoint is:
    (a) I hear what you're saying.
    (b) I see what you mean.

16. If I could choose only one of the following, I would sooner study:
    (a) language.
    (b) art.

HOW TO SCORE THE ASSESSMENT:

Total up all the (a)s and (b)s ticked for statements 1–8.
   Do the same for the (a)s and (b)s ticked for statements 9–16.

WHAT THE ASSESSMENT TELLS YOU

The first nine questions were adapted from the research of educational researcher and computer scientist Gordon Pask.[8] After analysing the performance of volunteers involved in a series of specially designed learning tasks, he discovered that they tended to use one of two very different approaches.

While both could prove equally effective, Pask also found that when there was a match between an individual's learning style and the way a subject had been structured, the task was accomplished far more easily and successfully than when a mismatch occurred. He called these two styles 'holist' and 'serialist'.

Your responses to statements 1–8 of the assessment will tell you which of these styles applies to you. I shall explain what answers to statements 9–16 revealed later in this chapter.

If you scored a majority of (a) responses, you are a Holist.

If you scored a majority of (b) responses, you are a Serialist.

These two can be viewed as end-points on a continuum:

Holist————————Serialist

The higher your total, the more likely it is that this style dominates your approach to formal learning. Most people lie at either end of the line, although a few are sufficiently flexible to adjust their learning style according to the demands of the task. It is still likely, however, that they feel most comfortable and learn best in just one of the two styles.

Let's examine each of the styles in turn, and explore their strengths and possible weaknesses. I shall then show you how, by appropriately organizing the information to be learnt, you can significantly increase your speed and efficiency when mastering an unfamiliar subject.

The Holist Approach to Learning

This learning style means that you prefer to obtain an overview of the subject right at the start and then fill in the details as you go along. You seek out general principles rather than focusing in on specific aspects of the topic, and you relate new ideas to ones already learnt.

HOW HOLISTS LEARN MOST EFFICIENTLY

You will do best in an unstructured learning situation. Because you are able to bring together a wide range of information, your approach is likely to prove most effective when there is a need to take an all-round approach to the subject.

Start by studying general concepts and develop a clear understanding of the broader issues before focusing on the fine detail. Since your natural learning style will cause you automatically to form a host of mental associations among a wide variety of ideas and concepts, the best approach is to plunge straight in at the deep end without spending too much time on preparation.

You should, however, create a fairly simple plan that will ensure that all the wider issues are fully examined and that you do not ignore any essential information.

There is a tendency among Holists to excel at the overview but to be on less firm ground when it comes to the fine detail.

This approach is termed 'top-down learning', and I shall describe the exact procedures in greater detail below.

When engaged in self-organized courses of study, you will normally find it a fairly simple matter to structure your learning in the way I have suggested. You may find yourself at a disadvantage, however, when following a course in which others have designed the study schedule. Manuals, textbooks and similar material in which facts build logically one on another may also make learning difficult. You may find yourself frustrated by having to move step by step through an operation's manual or the tutorial of a software package, and you will constantly try to jump ahead.

Help yourself by imposing as much structure as possible on the organization of the material. Develop your own summaries and signposts that will help you to see how each item ties in to the next, in order to help build associations between them. Create your own glossary of terms, an index, explanatory captions to the figures and alternative explanations of difficult concepts.

TOP-DOWN LEARNING

This involves a considerable overlap between topics, with several aspects of the subject being studied at the same time. As I have explained, your brain works best when it is allowed to form mental links and associations among various items of information. This insight will enable you to develop a powerful learning scheme by which any new material can be mastered easily and successfully.

To demonstrate how you can set about creating such a scheme, let us take just four topics which have to be learnt. You can, of course, use exactly the same approach for any number of topics. This is illustrated in Figure 4.1.

In the past you might have tried to learn these topics one after the other, like placing bricks on top of one another when building a house.

Research by Professor Pask, and my own twenty years' experience in helping people of all ages to learn more efficiently, suggests this seemingly

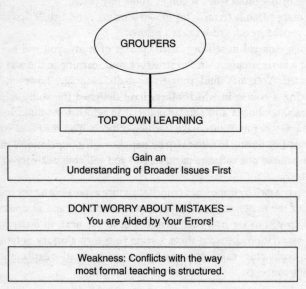

Figure 4.1 *'Top-down learning'*

common-sense approach actually makes it harder for you to remember the topics!

As a Holist, your best results will be obtained by learning Topics One and Two separately, before rehearsing them together. Repeat the exercise for Topics Three and Four, rehearsing the information they contain together in the same way.

Return to the first two items, and in your mind go through the information they contain, then carry out the same recall procedure on Topics Three and Four. Conclude by rehearsing all four topics together.

You can continue to study any number of topics by selecting four more and repeating the process. Organize the material in this way until either all the material you need to learn has been mastered or that particular study period comes to an end.

Always keep in mind these rules:

1. Start by obtaining an overall understanding of the big picture. Gain an insight into the general principles behind the topic before attempting to learn specific aspects.
2. Organize your study programme according to the Top-down learning plan as shown above. These two strategies will ensure that your studies are organized in such a way that they match perfectly the natural learning style of your brain.

The Serialist Approach to Learning

As a Serialist you will learn most efficiently by following a subject's logical progression from start to finish, in a systematic and methodical manner. You have a passion for detail and prefer to remain tightly focused on the topic under study.

HOW SERIALISTS LEARN MOST SUCCESSFULLY

If you scored higher on (b) than (a) statements in questions 1–8 of the assessment above, your preferred learning style is to use systematic and methodical study. You are fortunate, since this is the approach most frequently used in formal training and teaching courses.

On the other hand, you may feel a good deal less happy when faced with self-organized study, where the structure may be less clear and may demand a more holistic approach. My research suggests that uncertainty over how best to proceed may cause considerable anxiety – which, of course, impedes learning.

Your best approach under such circumstances is to set yourself clearly defined goals that make it easier to accumulate knowledge in a step-by-step manner. The way to do this is through Basement-up learning.

BASEMENT-UP LEARNING

As the name suggests, this involves proceeding methodically from one topic to the next, moving forward only when the current material has been fully understood.

If you are on a formal study or training programme, get hold of a detailed schedule of the topics to be covered and their order, then develop them into a Basement-up learning timetable as shown in Figure 4.2, below. By adopting such a structure, you should be able to double or treble your learning efficiency.

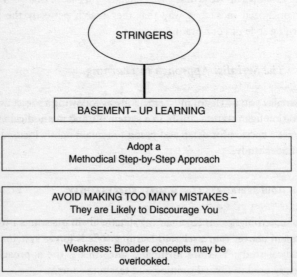

Figure 4.2 *'Basement-up learning'*

As the illustration shows, start by learning the first two topics separately then go over them together. Now study the third topic before going over all three of them together.

Study Topic Four and then go over all four topics once again in your mind. Continue to build your knowledge of the subject in this way, by treating the next topic as if it was Topic One and repeating the study sequence.

As I have already mentioned, your preferred style of learning gives you an advantage in most areas of formal study because it matches the way most training and teaching courses are structured. Because your mind excels at grasping specific details and forming links between facts, there is a risk that you may overlook broader concepts. Avoid this hazard by noting down any general principles and overall concepts that will need to be studied once you have gathered a significant body of knowledge on the subject.

While nobody enjoys making mistakes, Gordon Pask has shown that this is more likely to undermine the confidence and motivation of Serialists than of Holists. For this reason it is important for you to minimize the risk of making mistakes by adopting a procedure known as Progressive Fragmentation (PF). I shall be describing this powerful approach to learning in greater detail below.

By making sure that every step you take along the road to knowledge matches your stride, you avoid taking a humiliating tumble. Thus you prevent a fall which, the evidence suggests, could even make you doubt your ability ever to master that subject.

Progressive Fragmentation enables you to create stepping-stones that are wide enough apart to ensure progress is made, but are not separated so far as to make the journey hazardous.

As a Serialist, follow these two basic rules:

1. Construct your knowledge systematically. Start with specific facts and try to understand general concepts only after you have acquired a detailed grasp of fundamentals.
2. Organize your study schedule according to the Basement-up learning plan and use the rehearsal sequences described above.

Visualizer or Verbalizer?

Let us now return to the assessment and consider your score on statements 9–16. This explored the extent to which you are either a 'Visualizer' (more (a) than (b) responses ticked) or a 'Verbalizer' (more (b) than (a) responses ticked).

As with Holists and Serialists, these two approaches lie on a continuum.

Verbalizer————————————Visualizer

The higher your total for either letter, the more strongly this aspect of learning influences you. As with learning styles, these different approaches must be taken into account when you are learning.

HOW VISUALIZERS LEARN BEST

If you are a Visualizer, picturing ideas will assist in your learning and your concepts, so make use of all kinds of images, including flow-charts, diagrams, graphs, sketches, photographs and drawings. The more visual you are able to make the information, the easier you will find it to learn.

HOW VERBALIZERS LEARN BEST

If you are a Verbalizer, you prefer to listen, debate, argue, read, write and work one-on-one with your teacher. Discuss any problems or ideas with colleagues or other students. If there is nobody else to share your thoughts with, try talking them into a tape-recorder. The more you can verbalize the information, the easier you will find it is to learn.

Doers and Dreamers

There is one final aspect of learning that needs to be considered before we start looking at practical strategies for learning more successfully. This is the difference between those who prefer doing the hard work in their heads, the 'Dreamers', and those who favour learning via hands-on experience, the 'Doers'.

Einstein was a classic 'dreamer' who would perform complex experiments in his thoughts inside his head to inform himself as to how the real world worked. This may be why, when asked where his laboratory was, he is said to have picked up his fountain pen and responded simply: 'It is here!' American inventor Thomas Edison was a prime 'doer' whose lifetime of discovery involved the highly practical 'just do it' approach towards problem-solving. 'Edison held brave, if not cranky theories,' says Kevin Kelly, executive editor of *Wired* magazine. 'Nothing was as valuable to him as a working "demo" of an invention.'⁹ This is not to imply that Einstein was impractical and that Edison never reflected before acting. The difference is one of a preferred style of approach.

When striving to understand an unfamiliar idea or proposal, you may prefer to think long and hard. Arthur Conan Doyle's great detective Sherlock Holmes was a master of such deep thought. In *The Red-Headed League*, he says of a particular perplexing mystery: 'It is quite a three-pipe problem.'

Equally, you may find it much easier to come to an understanding if you can physically handle and manipulate materials.

Very few of us are, in fact, either total doers or total dreamers; we place ourselves somewhere between the two, depending on the type of problems or decisions with which we are concerned.

Unfortunately for doers, while either approach – or a combination of the two – is equally effective, it is the dreamers who are most likely to be regarded as intellectually gifted. This is especially true of much early education where, under the powerful influence of university learning, there is a tendency to dismiss practical people as less intelligent than abstract thinkers.

If you were caught in this trap early on in your education and, as a result, concluded that certain subjects were beyond your ability, take heart. Your approach to learning via doing can prove just as successful when tackling real-world problems as are the reflective thought-processes of the dreamers.

CREATING LEARNING LINKS

Have you ever had the experience of finding an answer by forgetting the question? It happened to me not long ago when I was struggling to bring to mind the name of a psychologist I had met several years previously while attending an international educational conference at Tarrytown, outside New York. Try as I might, his name remained elusive. I could almost recall it, but not quite – something psychologists call a TOT or 'tip-of-the-tongue' phenomenon.

After a while I gave up and turned my mind to more urgent matters. Before long I had, apparently, forgotten the question. The following morning I woke up with the psychologist's name clearly in my mind. It was Mel Kershansky and we had enjoyed an animated discussion about the importance of cerebral dominance. With the recollection of his name came a host of associated memories. I recalled in considerable detail the room in which we had held our discussions. I remembered the features of the young waitress who had served us coffee. The heated debate which followed Mel's presentation also came to mind, as did the fact that a mutual friend had taken a ridiculous picture of the two of us hamming it up for the camera. Later that day, to check my recollections, I dug through a pile of old snaps and even found the picture in question. It was almost, but not entirely, as I had recalled it.

All this illustrates a number of important points about learning, forgetting and remembering. I deal with the fallibility of memory later in this chapter. For the moment, I just want to draw your attention to two important features about the way we learn. The first concerns the TOT phenomenon and the fact that, even when you have dismissed a query from the level of awareness, part of your brain may continue searching for the answer. Like an industrious filing-clerk, it goes on opening drawers and shuffling through files until it comes up either with the right answer or with one that seems sufficiently close to the correct answer to warrant bringing it into your awareness. You may have noticed, for instance, that when hunting for a name like, say, 'Browning' several similar-sounding names, such as 'Brunning' or 'Breaching', may pop into your mind first. You know these are not quite right, but they are close to the desired answer. It's as if our industrious filing-clerk has located the right drawer in the correct cabinet, but has pulled out the wrong files.

The second point is that everything we hold in our memory, every single fact and figure, each event, incident and recollection that has been lodged there, is linked to everything else. Sometimes the links are short and easily made. By remembering Mel Kershansky's name, for instance, I instantly recalled a host of other associations: the room where we met, the discussions we had had and highlights from his presentation.

You can explore your own learning net by simply focusing on a single incident or event, a person's face, some remark you overheard, even a single word. Instantly you will be transported down memory lane, as associated ideas and recollections come flooding back.

For Marcel Proust, the taste of lime tea and a Madeleine biscuit were so powerful they triggered a chain of associations that led to his thirteen-volume autobiographical classic, *A la recherche du temps perdu*.

There are occasions when these links can lead us into error. If you'd like to demonstrate this – it makes a slight but amusing party trick – ask someone to answer the following questions as quickly as possible:

What is a common abbreviation for Coca-Cola?

Which word describes an amusing story told by a comedian?

What sound does a frog make on a lily pad?

What's the white of an egg called?

If they answer quickly enough, the chances are the responses will be: 'Coke – joke – croak – yolk!'

Perhaps that's how you responded to the questions. But, of course, the final answer is wrong. It should be 'albumen'.

What happened here was that, searching for a pattern among the seemingly disconnected questions, your brain hit on the idea of looking for rhymes. This caused 'yolk' to seem the obviously correct response, whereas a moment's thought would have shown that this was wrong.

One of the first to recognize these mental links was the seventeenth-century English philosopher, John Locke, in his treatise *An Essay concerning Human Understanding*. He proposed that ideas become associated in our minds as a result of a natural relationship or by chance or through habit. As a result, he wrote, these ideas 'always keep in company, and the one no sooner at any time comes into the understanding, but its associate appears with it'.[10]

At its most basic, this simply means that information that makes sense is easier to learn and recall than information that makes no sense at all. This can be demonstrated by a piece of deliberate nonsense, written by

Samuel Foote, an English wit and actor, in order to test the boasted memory of a fellow thespian, the Irish actor Charles Macklin. See how difficult, or easy, you find memorizing the following:

So she went into the garden to cut a cabbage leaf, to make an apple-pie; and at the same time a great she-bear, coming up the street, pops its head into the shop. 'What! No soap?' So he died, and she very imprudently married the barber; and there were present the Picinnies, and the Joblillies, and the Garyalies, and the great Panjandrum himself, with the little round button at top, and they all fell to playing the game of catch-as-catch-can, till the gunpowder ran out at the heels of their boots.[11]

The difficulty in remembering these few lines of prose lies in the fact that the brain cannot easily organize them, since there are no logical connections between the lines.

In a series of experiments designed to explore our networks of knowledge, two American psychologists, Doctors Allen Collins and Ross Quillian, of the University of California,[12] measured the time taken to decide whether or not statements were true or false. They reported that the speed with which decisions were made depended on the degree of association between the concepts concerned. When the association was close, subjects answered almost instantly, while a less direct relationship increased the time taken to reply. When asked to say whether or not a canary was 'yellow', for example, people responded immediately and correctly. But asked to say whether or not a canary was an animal, they took longer to answer.

If we imagine these two ideas, 'yellow' and 'is an animal', as items in a knowledge network, as illustrated in Figure 4.3, the reasons for these time differences become apparent.

As with any other journey, when the distance to be travelled is short, our trips down memory lane are faster and there is less risk of getting lost along the way. Equally, the further the distance, the more time is needed to complete the journey and the greater is the risk of taking a wrong turning. In order to recall new information rapidly and accurately therefore, information must be organized in such a way that relevant items are linked together by the shortest possible pathways through the network.

Three types of evidence support the idea that such organization is important for successful learning:

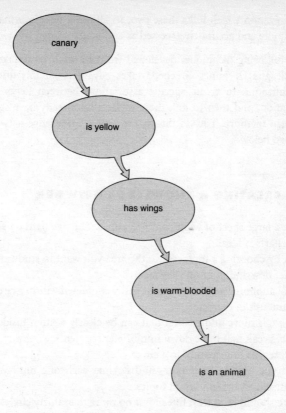

Figure 4.3 *'Time needed to search knowledge network'*

1. Demonstrations that such material is far easier to remember than disorganized information.
2. Evidence that, when provided with disorganized information, people spontaneously attempt to organize it.
3. Research which shows that instructions to organize new information significantly enhance learning.[13]

Such organization exists at three levels:

1. Knowledge already organized in long-term memory.
2. The organization perceived or generated within the material to be learnt.

3. Organization which links these two, so allowing new information to be rapidly and accurately accessed as and when needed.

The following technique, developed from research undertaken with my colleague Dr James Greene,[14] takes advantage of this third level of organization to create specific associations between items of new information, and then to link these to facts we already have stored in long-term memory. You do this by creating a 'knowledge network', as described below.

CREATING A KNOWLEDGE NETWORK

- Take a large sheet of white, unlined paper. The size used on standard flip-charts is ideal.
- Start by choosing a topic within the area you want to study and write a brief description of one key fact.
- Write no more words than can be easily contained within a circle eight centimetres in diameter.
- If there is more information that can be clearly written inside such a circle, break that topic down into briefer segments.
- Enclose this information in a circle.
- Continue writing brief notes and circling each one until you have exhausted all the important topics.
- There should be at least fifteen but no more than thirty circles in your network.
- Select an item of information that appears to be a logical starting point for creating the network. Choose the one that is most familiar to you, since this will imply that it is associated with knowledge already in your long-term memory.
- Identify a second circle containing facts that are logically related to the first one selected. It makes no difference whereabouts on the sheet it is, just so long as you personally can form a logical association between the two.
- Join these circles with a line.
- Select a third circle containing information that you can logically relate to the second one selected. Join these two circles with a line.
- Continue in this way until all the circles are linked together. This

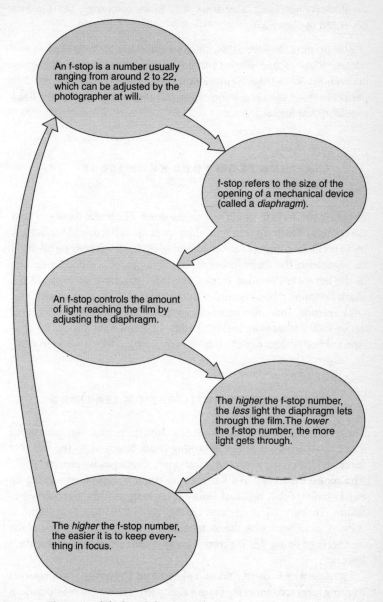

Figure 4.4 *'The knowledge network'*

should leave you with a network that looks something like the one illustrated in Figure 4.4.

Bear in mind, however, that, since we each have an individual way of relating ideas to one another, there may be considerable differences between the Knowledge Network you create and one made by another person learning the same information. All that matters is that the links should appear logical to you.

LEARNING FROM YOUR KNOWLEDGE NETWORK

There are two ways in which this can be done. The first is simply to read the content of each circle in turn, then cover up all but one of them. Now try to recall the content of either adjoining circle. Check your recollection by uncovering that circle before repeating the process with the next one in the network. Continue in this way until you have gone round the whole network and can remember the contents of all the circles accurately.

The second, and rather more efficient, method is to construct a simple device called a 'memory maker'. Before I explain how this can be constructed from a sheet of stiff card, let's take a look at why it works so well.

THE POWER OF ANTICIPATION LEARNING

The traditional image of the industrious learner, poring over books with a wet towel wrapped round an aching head, blinds us to the fact that successful learning is always an active rather than a passive process. Those who regard their brain as a bio-chemical sponge, capable of soaking up any knowledge that is placed before it for long enough, are doomed to failure. To learn effectively and reliably recall what has been learnt, it is essential to work with the material in a dynamic manner. One of the best ways of doing this is through an approach known as 'anticipation learning'.

Developed by Richard Atkinson of Stanford University,[15] anticipation learning takes account of the brain's ability to make extensive associations and to file items under a variety of headings. Professor Atkinson's research has shown that this method can be used to master any subject. The key to anticipation learning is to use one item to provide clues to the next. By repeated use of this method, the brain develops links between the ideas so that the presentation of just one piece of information enables you accurately to recall all the related topics.

The Memory Maker, described below, is a method for making this method faster and easier by automating it.

CONSTRUCTING A MEMORY MAKER

The exact dimensions of the Memory Maker depend on the extent of your Knowledge Network. Many of the executives to whom I have taught this technique over the past decade, however, prefer to create much larger knowledge networks using flip-chart-size sheets of white paper. The dimensions given below are intended for use with such large-size networks.

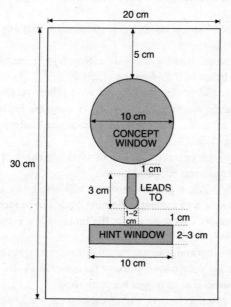

Figure 4.5 *'The Memory Maker'*

- Five centimetres from the top edge of the card cut out a circle ten centimetres in diameter. This is the concept window.
- One centimetre below the lower edge of the concept window cut a key-hole shape, three centimetres long and one to two centimetres wide. This is the 'leads to' guide. Its purpose is to enable you to line one circle up with the next by means of the linking line. The exact dimensions will depend on the size of the circles in your network. The concept window should be sufficiently large to show all the notes written in each individual circle.
- The final step is to produce a flap one to two centimetres beneath the bottom of the 'leads to' guide. Cut this on three sides and fold it back along the top edge. This is the 'hint window'.

Your Memory Maker (see Figure 4.5) is now ready for use with your Knowledge Networks.

USING THE MEMORY MAKER

- Position the Memory Maker's concept window over any circle on the network.
- Read out the information it contains. Now try to remember the information in either of the adjoining circles.
- If you are confident that the information has been recalled completely and accurately, slide the Memory Maker along the linking line, using the 'leads to' guide, and check by reading the contents through the concept window.
- If you are unable to remember exactly what is in either of the adjoining circles, then take an educated guess.
- Keeping the circle within the concept window, rotate the card until the line linking it to the next adjoining circle can be seen through the 'leads to' guide. This ensures that the hint window is positioned over the next circle.
- Push up the flap and read the partial information revealed. Use this as a 'hint' to jog your memory about the entire contents. Usually all it takes is a small clue to trigger accurate recall.
- Check your recollections by sliding the concept window over that circle and reading out the information.

- Now try to remember the information in the next circle on the network.
- Continue in this way until you return to your starting point. After only a couple of trips around the network, you should find it easy to remember all the information it contains. Furthermore, because you have learnt it as a network, rather than as a list, it is possible to begin anywhere in the net and return to your starting point. This means that, by remembering the contents of any circle, the whole network can be reconstructed.

Because you chose your own starting point when creating the network, the information in that first circle will already be linked to items in long-term memory. In this way you will be forming a secure bridge from information already established in long-term memory to the new information that you have to learn.

To ensure that this combination of Knowledge Network and Memory Maker works most efficiently, keep the following points in mind.

- Move around the network in one direction only. After reading the contents of the first circle, move to either of the adjoining ones. But having made that move, whether clockwise or anticlockwise, you must continue around the network in the same direction.
- Ensure that you understand everything written in a circle. Not only will any ambiguity or misunderstanding make it harder to remember and recall that information, it will also introduce a weakness into the network.
- If you intend to use the network with a Memory Maker, it is helpful to draft the network using the card as a template, prior to writing any notes. This ensures that all the information is included within the appropriate area.

PROGRESSIVE FRAGMENTATION

At school, perhaps you were compelled to learn by rote a topic that seemed completely incomprehensible. When you made a mistake, you had no clear idea why; if you happened, by lucky accident, to come up with a correct answer, you still didn't know why that response was right. These experiences are certainly not confined to childhood. Adults too are often faced with the need to learn a topic about which they have little or no understanding. Such situations pose the most painful and discouraging of all learning tasks.

It cannot be emphasized too much that in order to learn successfully you must fully understand what it is you are learning.

This may strike you as a paradox, since most people assume that understanding is the result, not the driving force, of learning. They are seriously mistaken. If you drum into your brain a piece of information that makes no sense to you, not only will this be harder to recall but it is likely to undermine all subsequent information that builds on that misunderstood notion. Like a building constructed on shaky foundations, your house of knowledge will be in grave risk of tumbling down.

The key to understanding a big idea is to break it into smaller and smaller pieces, the process I term 'progressive fragmentation' (PF). While there are problems that may appear, at first sight, extremely difficult to understand, just as there are subjects that *look* very complex when first examined, the great majority can be broken down into components that can be understood.

If you fail to make sense of something, break the topic down into simpler elements. Still baffled? Then fragment those elements still further. Continue in this way until a point is reached at which the meaning becomes clear.

Once this moment of insight has been achieved, your understanding will work its way back up the sequence of ideas, instantly resolving your initial source of confusion.

Learning, as I have pointed out, is no longer an optional extra for adult life but an absolute essential for anyone with the ambition to progress through their chosen profession or career. As adults, already pressured into keeping ahead of an ever-growing workload, the prospect of finding sufficient free time to set aside for such studying can be daunting – so daunting that the majority of people seldom tackle it. The fact that you have been sufficiently interested in ways of using your mind more efficiently, and are sufficiently concerned about information overload to do something about it, suggests that you are not among that majority.

By using the insights into your personal learning style that this chapter has provided, and by making use of the practical study procedures I have described, the task of lifelong learning can be transformed from a worrying burden into an enjoyable and stress-free challenge.

SUMMARY

- We each have a personal learning style that determines the way in which new information can be acquired most easily and comfortably.
- Some people are Holists and prefer to gain an overview of the topic before focusing in on the finer details.
- Others are Serialists, and they prefer to learn via a logical progression, building one fact on the next and focusing on the details in order to create an overall understanding of the subject.
- By matching your personal learning style to the way in which information is presented, you will find it far easier to master unfamiliar topics.
- If you favour a Holist approach, then use Top-down learning.
- If you favour a Serialist approach, then use Basement-up learning.
- Another important difference in the way people learn is between those who do best when they can visualize the information and those who prefer to listen and discuss.
- The final difference between various kinds of learners is between action and abstraction. Dreamers like to work with ideas, while doers want to roll up their sleeves and learn through direct experience. Neither approach is superior to the other but, by using the method you find most comfortable, learning is achieved more rapidly and easily.
- Tie information together by creating learning links. In the mind, these consist of forming clear associations between the different items to be learnt, while on paper they comprise a written-out 'knowledge network'. Use the easily constructed Memory Maker device to learn all the facts in a network in the shortest possible time and with the greatest degree of accurate recall.
- Finally, never try to learn anything you do not fully understand. Use 'progressive fragmentation' to break down complex and poorly understood topics into smaller and more manageable elements that make complete sense to you.

Build Yourself a Better Memory

'But each day brings its petty dust
Our soon-chok'd souls to fill,
And we forget because we must,
And not because we will.'

                                        Matthew Arnold, *Absence* (1857)

In 1981, during the Watergate investigation of Richard Nixon, his counsel John Dean was apparently able to recall, in fine detail, a great number of conversations between himself and the President. So faultless did these recollections appear that Dean was dubbed The Human Tape-Recorder. Dean was certain he could remember the conversations almost verbatim. Yet when recordings of the actual conversations were revealed, it immediately became apparent that, while he had got the content of conversations roughly correct, the actual words and style employed were very different.[1] John Dean's fallibility reminds us what a hazardous business it can be to trust to our memory, especially when deluged with data as a result of information overload.

As I explained in Chapter Three, the facts about which we feel most certain often turn out to have been misremembered, and with gaps between the reliable recollections filled in by confabulations. Yet, as Matthew Arnold pointed out, forgetting is as essential as remembering. If we were unable to forget anything and could recall in perfect detail everything that happened, no matter how trivial, living would become a perpetual anguish.

Some of the difficulties we would face in these circumstances are illustrated by the story of Shereshevskii, a Moscow journalist during the

1920s. Shereshevskii never forgot anything: he remembered all that he saw and heard, down to the smallest detail, from the most significant events to the most trivial. If he glanced at a railway timetable just once, for example, he could recall every departure and destination with absolute accuracy thirty years later.

Shereshevskii's incredible memory first came to public attention when his editor noticed that, without ever taking any notes, he could repeat, word for word, all the instructions he was given. The editor sent him to Moscow University to see the neuropsychologist Alexandr Romanovich Luria. It was the start of a lifelong professional relationship, during which Luria intensively studied Shereshevskii's powers, finally writing a fascinating book about him, *The Mind of a Mnemonist*.[2]

As an illustration of Shereshevskii's astonishing memory, consider the following meaningless formula:

$$N. \sqrt{\frac{d^2 \cdot x\,85.}{vx}} \quad \sqrt{\frac{276^2 \cdot 86x.\ n^2b}{n^2v \cdot \pi264}}$$

After studying this confusion of letters, numbers and mathematical symbols for only a few minutes, Shereshevskii was able to reproduce it perfectly. Not only that, but when he was tested, without advance warning, thirty years later, he was again able to write it down without a single error. 'There seemed to be no limit either to the capacity of his memory or to the durability of the traces he retained,' says psychologist Richard Gross. 'He could recall, without error, a list of words that increased up to thirty, fifty and even seventy, and he could remember nonsense material after days, months or even years.'[3]

In part, Shereshevskii was able to perform these seemingly impossible feats of memory by using visual imagery, a valuable technique when coping with information overload, as I shall explain in detail in a moment. Although he became a successful stage performer, delighting the public with incredible feats of memory, his gift seems to have been as much a curse as a blessing, and one which adversely affected his life in many ways. 'His tendency to remember everything in terms of mental images often prevented him from grasping abstract concepts,' notes Professor Alan Parkin of the University of Sussex.[4] 'He was also hindered by his inability to forget. Problems arose when he began to confuse the information he had just committed to memory with that from previous performances.'

In the end, Shereshevskii solved some of these problems by devising an ingenious way to forget. He imagined the information he wanted to remove from his memory being written on a blackboard, and then he saw himself rubbing it out. Unlikely as it may seem, this method worked and, perhaps for the first time in his life, the Russian possessed a skill the rest of us take for granted and often regret – the ability to forget!

When it comes to infoglut, the controlled *forgetting* of inessential information, combined with the accurate and reliable recording of essential facts and figures, are crucial survival skills.

DECIDING WHAT YOU NEED TO REMEMBER

Before committing anything to memory, adopt the same approach as I suggested in Chapter Four for reading. Ask yourself the following questions.

Why exactly should I bother to remember this information? When, where, why and how will I use it? Over what time period will I need to remember it? With what accuracy will I have to recall it?

You can also use a similar formula for calculating the usefulness of any material before bothering to commit it to memory:

$$\text{Usefulness of memory} = \frac{\text{Relevance} \times \text{Accuracy}}{\text{Work required memorizing}}$$

If you don't need to remember something, then do not waste time and effort in doing so.

If the information has to be retained, identify the best method for storing it, balancing the time taken to do so against the timescale over which it must be retained, the frequency with which it will be consulted and the ease with which it can be accessed.

A scribbled note may be quick and convenient, provided the information is going to be accessed within a short space of time (trying to make sense of a terse *aide-mémoire* even as little as a week after the event is often all but impossible!).

Books, journals and printed reports enjoy a longer lifespan, although retrieving just the fact or figure needed from a lengthy text is often tedious and time-consuming.

Electronic devices offer far easier retrieval, especially when their software allows you to go straight to any particular portion of the text. On the other hand, getting information into electronic storage in the first place, even when documents are scanned into the system, is more time-consuming.

Ask yourself the following questions. Why is a particular item being stored? When and under what circumstances is it likely to be used? Will the person who wants to recover that information be the same one who placed it in store originally? If not, will he or she understand the codes used to identify it?

Most computer-users have wasted considerable time trying to track down an elusive file that they 'know' is somewhere in the system, yet which they cannot bring to light. Even with the assistance of software tools like Microsoft Explorer or the 'Find' command within Windows '95, finding what you want can prove frustrating and, occasionally, futile. This is especially likely to happen if someone other than you has stored the information, whether as a paper document or a digital record.

Use your memory to retain just that information which will need to be accessed rapidly and when complete accuracy is *not* the main consideration. For, with the rare exceptions of men and women like Shereshevskii, the human brain has not evolved to create photographic records of all we see and hear. Its purpose is, rather, to set down fleeting impressions of events, especially those associated with powerful emotions. This is why some of our most enduring recollections include shocking news, such as President Kennedy's assassination or the death of Princess Diana, as well as more trivial but equally moving incidents: a brilliant sunset, the first meeting with a lover, an act of kindness from a stranger. As Stephen Pinker puts it: '. . . the limits of memory are not a by-product of a mushy storage medium. As programmers like to say, "It's not a bug, it's a feature." '[5]

Unfortunately, in today's information-rich world, great accuracy is often demanded in the way facts and figures are recalled. Computers are sensitive to any deviance; lawyers keep a close watch for mistakes; and a simple blunder can cost your company millions. All of which means that on those occasions when we have no option but to depend on memory, special strategies must be used to ensure that retention and recall are as reliable and speedy as possible. It is with such strategies for enhancing memory that the rest of this chapter is concerned.

HOW INFORMATION OVERLOAD MAKES US FORGET

There are three barriers to retaining and recalling new material when struggling with the burden of overload.

Barrier No. 1: Recollection is insufficiently robust.

Barrier No. 2: New memories disrupt older ones.

Barrier No. 3: Anxiety caused by a lack of confidence in our memory creates a self-fulfilling prophecy.

Let us consider practical strategies for overcoming each of these barriers.

Barrier No. 1: Recollection is insufficiently robust

Human memory has three storage areas. This first, called the *sensory store*, holds information for only a fraction of a second. The second, short-term or working memory, holds a larger but still limited amount of information for up to twenty seconds. The third is long-term storage, where we house a lifetime of memories.

The limited capacity of working memory was first discussed, more than forty years ago, in a paper by George Miller with the intriguing title 'The magical number seven, plus or minus two: Some limits on our capacity for processing information'.[6] In his paper, Miller showed that working memory has between five and nine slots (seven plus or minus two), each of which is capable of holding one unit, or bit, of information. This means the least amount of information people with normal memories can retain is five items, for example 56789, and the maximum is nine items, 234567897, with an average of seven items. This is why telephone numbers, without the area code, are usually limited to a maximum of nine digits, with most being around seven digits or fewer.

By *chunking* the information, however, many more than nine items can be remembered. The letters PSPSIMISSII would be tricky to remember, but when rearranged into Mississippi they occupy only one slot in working memory. American children are sometimes taught to spell this word by chunking it into three groups: MIS SIS SIPPI, and chanting it aloud. Try for yourself, and if you've ever had any trouble knowing how to spell the USA's twentieth state you never will again.

Why the 'magical number seven'? George Miller's tongue-in-cheek allusion referred to the fact that, in mythology and superstition, seven is believed to possess mystical properties. The seventh child is said to be especially lucky, for example, while the seventh son of a seventh son can foretell the future and cure disease.

From the point of view of using our memory more when faced with information overload, two important facts emerge: the first is that working memory holds only a small amount of information and for less than half a minute; the second is that, without adequate rehearsal to transfer it to long-term storage, that information will disappear beyond recall. The amount of attention paid to an event also affects short-term storage, and this in turn is determined by how personally relevant the information is.

By adopting the following schedule of rehearsal, both these limitations on remembering can easily be overcome.

HOW TO REMEMBER TWICE AS MUCH IN HALF THE TIME

Time, as most of us know to our cost, is not kind to memories. The further in the past something happened, the harder it gets to recall it to mind except in the sketchiest possible manner. If we were to draw a graph of how much is forgotten over different periods of time, it would look something like Figure 5.1.

As you can see, the line of forgetfulness sweeps smoothly down, revealing that, after only sixty minutes, quite a lot of information has been lost; three days later, forgetting levels off at around 90 per cent which means that we can recall only 10 per cent of what we hoped to remember.

Now imagine that the graph could be turned upside down, so that it looks like Figure 5.2.

As you can see, the amount recalled actually *increases* as time passes, with a peak being reached some two days after learning took place. In this case, we have achieved an enrichment of recall in the same proportion as the previous memory loss.

That such a reversal of the normal forgetting curve can be achieved was first demonstrated by Doctors Matthew Erdelyi and James Kleinbard of the City University of New York.[7] In their studies, volunteers were

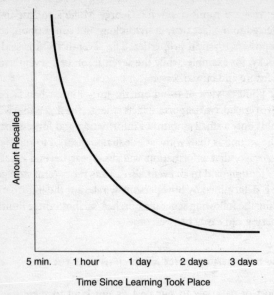

Figure 5.1 *'Graph of forgetting'*

taught to recall twice as much information the day after they had memorized some material as they achieved just five minutes afterwards.

Here's how it works. Imagine you are attending a meeting where, although it is not practicable to make written notes, you need to remember accurately all the key points discussed. As the meeting progresses, make a mental note of the major topics by repeating them silently to yourself. You also need to keep a running total of *how many* points you will wish to recall. One way of doing this is simply to make a tick on a sheet of scrap paper each time an important topic arises; another is to transfer a series of coins from one pocket to another.

Exactly *five minutes* after the meeting has finished, find a quiet place where you can sit down, relax and spend no more than a couple of minutes mentally running over those main points. Repeat each topic to yourself just once. If you have the chance of jotting down a brief note on each topic, then do so, since this will enhance memory even further. But if there is no such opportunity, this does not much matter. Immediately after the recall session you should in any event discard these notes, since it is the action of writing them down that makes the memory more robust.

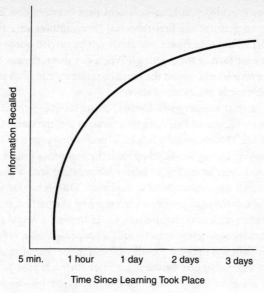

Figure 5.2 *'Graph of remembering'*

Do not be concerned if, even during that brief lapse of time, quite a lot of information seems to have gone missing. Make an educated guess about anything you cannot readily bring to mind, but never strain to recall elusive items.

Rehearsal session number two takes place *one hour* after the meeting. As before, simply go through each item and repeat it to yourself just once. Stay relaxed and if you can't seem to bring an item to mind, take an educated guess. Never strain to remember or start feeling anxious about what is only a temporary memory lapse. Rehearse twice more in an identical manner, once *three hours* after the meeting and a final time *six hours* later, or at bedtime, whichever is the sooner.

During the days that follow, have two or three rehearsal sessions, spread evenly throughout the day. From then on you will be able to keep the memories fresh by rehearsing them every three or four days. There is never any need to try to repeat each item in its entirety as a few key words to remind you of the topic are all that is necessary.

If you attended a number of meetings, all within a short time of one another, the same technique can be used to reinforce key memories for each meeting. Provided you have sufficient time between one meeting and the next to perform the first rehearsal (five minutes after the first meeting ends) all the subsequent rehearsals can be carried out as before, only this time for each of the meetings. When one meeting runs directly on from the previous one, count the two as a single meeting and perform the rehearsals exactly as described above.

To improve your memory still further, create mental pictures of key ideas. The more bizarre and striking these images are, the easier they are to bring to mind. This is especially helpful in preventing your recollections from one meeting getting muddled up with the memories from a second which followed soon after. Try to label each meeting with a particular image and attach the memories to that picture. One executive told me how he would cast the chairperson at each meeting as a particular animal. A very slow and ponderous chairperson, for example, he would imagine as a giant tortoise wearing spectacles and a toupee – which is how the human equivalent was dressed. Another he cast in the role of an alligator with a giant cigar clamped between his jaws. In each case he would visualize an image of the relevant beast before going into each of his rehearsal sessions; to recall the key points of a meeting, all he then needed to do was to bring to mind the right jungle creature, and all the recollections flooded clearly and accurately into his mind.

If you get stuck at any point, use a process of *free association* to help jog your memory. While remaining relaxed, think about the first thing that the last topic you clearly remember reminds you of. This will produce an association of some kind, and this can then be used to trigger a second association, and so on, until, after a number of links have been formed, the topic you need will re-emerge.

SUMMARY OF REHEARSAL SCHEDULE

- Make a note of the total number of topics to remember.
- Have your first rehearsal session five minutes after the event. Stay relaxed. Never strain after an elusive memory. Take educated guesses to fill in any gaps. Repeat each item just once.
- Session two comes after one hour, session three after three hours and session four six hours later, or at bedtime.
- Rehearse two or three times over the next couple of days. Spread the sessions throughout the day.

- Keep your memory of topics fresh by rehearsing every three or four days thereafter.
- Use vivid visual imagery to link ideas to a particular meeting.
- If two meetings run on one after the other, count them as a single session for the purposes of rehearsal.

Because there are individual differences in the way memories work, use the above schedule as a guide only. Compare the effectiveness of different rehearsal schedules, of using or not using imagery, or free association.

Barrier No. 2: New memories disrupt older ones

When something we have learnt *earlier* interferes with our memory of material learnt later, this is termed *proactive interference*. When something we have learnt *later* interferes with our memory for items learnt earlier, it is known as *retroactive interference*. Both proactive and retroactive interference are extremely common among information workers faced with a relentless flow of new facts and figures to understand. They may lead to what has been termed the 'Chinese Meal Syndrome', so called because it involves forgetting something within a short time of learning it. The effects of overshadowing due to overload can be reduced in a number of ways:

- As I suggested in Chapter Four, memorizing important information last thing at night and taking a break between periods of study makes for easier retention and more accurate recall.
- Over-learn the subject; that is to say, repeat it so many times that every item becomes deeply embedded in the memory.
- Use another memory store; for example, trying to remember a telephone number by repeating it to yourself when dialling can cause you either to misdial or forget the number. Instead, imagine the number written in bright red ink on pure white paper (for some reason this combination seems to aid recall) and see it floating in front of your eyes as you dial. By doing so, interference no longer poses a problem.
- If you forget a recently acquired memory, try going through the alphabet and considering each letter in turn. This may help trigger a key word or sentence.
- Counting from one to ten can have a similar effect to running through the alphabet.

- Try to mentally evoke the surroundings or situation in which the material was memorized.
- Use free association, by asking yourself what the last item you can clearly remember reminds you of. Then form a second association with that item, and so on.
- Avoid forcefully thinking about the elusive topic, and it is likely quite suddenly to pop into your head.

Barrier No. 3: Lack of confidence in our powers of memory

Despite the caution I have urged about placing too much trust in our memory, and given that, when trying to handle information overload, memory lapses become a virtual certainty, it is still vitally important to have faith in your powers of retention and recall.

Instead of accepting that memory lapses – even foolish and embarrassing ones – are unavoidable in busy people, many victims of forgetfulness use such slips as evidence that they are unable to remember even simple things. How often have you heard it said: 'I've got a terrible memory for names!' 'I've got a memory like a sieve!' 'I'd forget my own head if it wasn't screwed on tight!' Perhaps you've even voiced similar doubts yourself about your own memory. By doing so, one creates a self-fulfilling prophecy of forgetfulness, which makes it more likely that your memory will let you down in the future. Not only will you approach remembering with less confidence, but you will also feel far more anxious about meeting the challenge.

Since high levels of anxiety significantly impair memory function, as most of us know to our cost, such pessimistic prophecies are almost certain to come true.

DEVELOPING A POSITIVE ATTITUDE TOWARDS YOUR MEMORY

How confident do you feel about your memory? Would you rate it as excellent, average or poor? As I have just explained, a negative attitude creates a self-fulfilling prophecy of failure.

Check your own memory by reading through the four memory tests below. Before attempting any of them, decide how many you could carry out with at least 90 per cent accuracy. *I rate my chances of completing the four tests with 90 per cent accuracy as:* (a) zero to minimal; (b) fair to good; (c) excellent.

Memory Test One

Read through the twenty words below for one minute, then repeat them from memory, first from the start of the list forwards, then from the end of the list backwards.

Pumpkin, Aeroplane, Kitten, Dunce's cap, Harmonium, Jelly, Forest, Castle, Chariot, Rocking chair, Shotgun, Banquet, Stone, Bread, Cream, Ship, Snowmen, Television, Oak tree, Catapult

Memory Test Two

Write down and immediately recall a string of any fifty numbers of your own choosing.

Memory Test Three

Recall the following fifteen grocery items, in the correct order, having read the list just once.

Eggs, flour, cheese, bacon, apples, salt, cereals, mustard, sliced bread, bananas, pickles, milk, fish, washing-up liquid, orange juice

Now repeat the list in reverse order!

Memory Test Four

Recall the following nine-digit number after just one reading:

299,792.458

How well did you do?

(a) All four tests completed with 90 per cent accuracy or better.

(b) Three completed with 90 per cent accuracy or better.

(c) Two completed with 90 per cent accuracy or better.

(d) One completed with 90 per cent accuracy or better.

(e) Failed all four tests.

(f) Knew they were hopeless and did not waste my time attempting them.

The chances are your score was (c) (d) (e) or (f). If so, the negative opinion you probably have of your memory has been confirmed.

If you scored (a) or (b), my congratulations. I suggest you skip straight to the next chapter.

In fact, all these apparently difficult memory tests are extremely easy to perform. Once you know how to do them, you can amaze your friends by carrying out similar feats effortlessly and with 100 per cent accuracy.

How to Succeed with Memory Test One

What usually happens when you try to learn the list by reading through it several times is that you can remember the first few and the last few nouns without much difficulty, but you get badly muddled or completely lost around the middle. This is an example of the primary and recency effects in remembering: we recall best what we hear first and last.

One problem in mastering this list is that all the words are well known to you and are already stored in your long-term memory. Because they are not linked together, however, remembering one word, say 'bread', will not help bring to mind the words on either side of it: 'stone' and 'cream'.

Instead of trying to learn this as a list of words, create an image of each noun and then join these images together into a mind movie. This is the equivalent of forming the 'learning links' I described in Chapter Four.

Here is a suggested mind movie. Bear in mind that, because I have created the images and formed the links on your behalf, it will not prove as powerful as if it had been entirely your own creation. Even so, you should find it a relatively simple matter to go through the list forwards or backwards, or even to start somewhere in the middle and proceed in either direction.

MIND MOVIE FOR 'PUMPKIN' LIST

As you read through this movie script, conjure up as vividly as you possibly can the mental images I describe. Make each as bizarre as possible, with gigantic proportions and brilliant colours.

Imagine a giant *pumpkin*, a really huge one, the biggest pumpkin in the entire world.

This has been fitted with wings, jet engines and a tail to turn it into an *aeroplane*.

This strange aircraft is being flown by a *kitten*; try to picture it sitting behind the controls wearing a leather helmet and flying goggles.

The kitten is such a hopeless pilot that it is wearing a large, pointed *dunce's cap* with a big red 'D' drawn on the front.

As it flies the aircraft with one paw, the kitten is playing an old-fashioned *harmonium* with the other.

This is a very strange harmonium since it is made entirely of *jelly* – imagine the whole instrument wobbling as the kitten plays it.

Due to the kitten's inattention, the aircraft crash-lands in a deep, dark *forest*. Picture the rows and rows of pine trees.

Close by is a fabulous Disney-style *castle*, complete with turrets and battlements.

From within this castle comes the local ruler, riding out in an ornate golden *chariot*, on which is perched an old *rocking chair*.

Clutched in the ruler's hands is a double-barrelled *shotgun*.

The passengers are invited to a *banquet*; imagine a long table covered in a pure white damask cloth.

But the only food on offer is one very large *stone*. See a huge stone placed at the head of the table, ready to be served.

When the guests begin eating the stone, however, it turns magically into *bread*.

When the bread is sliced, a river of *cream* pours forth – so much cream in fact that a *ship* is sailing on it. (Imagine any vessel you like; into my mind's eye when writing this came the image of an old riverboat paddle-steamer, its great rear paddle turning slowly and black smoke billowing from four tall funnels.)

This ship is crewed by *snowmen*, who are all gathered round an ancient black-and-white *television* set whose aerial is an *oak tree*. Picture the tree growing up behind the set.

Instead of acorns, this tree is sprouting a crop of *catapults* which are busy hurling stones at a gigantic pumpkin flying overhead.

By associating the final image in your mind movie, 'catapult', with the first, 'pumpkin', you have turned the list into a loop, which means you can start anywhere and proceed in either direction around the loop, confidently and correctly recalling every single item.

Try this now, starting with 'Pumpkin . . .'

If you found that fairly easy, try going in reverse order around the loop, beginning with 'catapult, oak tree . . .' and so on.

Using images to aid the memory is an extremely old technique whose roots go back to ancient Greece. It is widely taught in 'memory enhancement' courses, sold through national newspapers and magazines. Although, as used here, it is little more than a parlour trick, two important lessons can be learnt from it: first, using images, especially bizarre ones, is a powerful way of boosting our memory in many situations; secondly, linking memories in a specific way makes it far easier to recall them all, once you have accessed one. I shall discuss this powerful technique further in a moment.

How to Succeed with Memory Test Two

The secret here is simply to write down any fifty digits that you have already learnt by heart; for example, most telephone numbers are at least eleven digits long; if you know five phone numbers – and the majority of people do – then you have achieved more than the target required. Link them together, and you produce a fifty-five-digit number. Add any other numbers you know – from your credit card, bank account, fax – and you could well extend that number to a hundred or even more.

There is nothing inherently difficult in recalling fifty numbers – it just sounds as if it's going to be!

How to Succeed with Memory Test Three

The fifteen-item shopping list can be learnt easily in one of two ways. The first is by creating a mind movie similar to that described for test one. The second is to make use of an equally ancient technique known as the method of *loci*; this was originally developed by Greek orators as a means of remembering speeches that could last many hours. What they did was to form an image of some familiar location, such as their own home, then take a mental tour of the location, placing the items to be remembered in imaginary positions.

In this case you might take a mental stroll around your home or office, placing items of shopping on various pieces of furniture. Imagine, for example, opening your front door and leaving six eggs on the hall table.

Entering the living room, you put a bag of flour on the occasional table and a slice of cheese on the TV. Rashers of bacon are laid on the mantelpiece, while you put some apples on an armchair and a packet of salt on the sofa.

Going into the dining room, you place a box of cereals on the sideboard and a jar of mustard on the table.

Climbing the stairs, you pause only to leave some sliced bread on the landing and a bunch of bananas outside the bathroom door.

A jar of pickles goes on your bed and a bottle of milk on the dressing table.

You place a fish in the bath, washing-up liquid on the lavatory seat and a container of orange juice in the shower cubicle.

Mentally position each item clearly in the chosen location and never re-enter a room to add another item once you have left it.

With very little practice you will find the method of *loci* an extremely reliable way of recalling miscellaneous items of information like this. To recover the list, merely retrace your steps around the location, in this example starting at your front door and picturing six eggs on the hall table.

To repeat the list in reverse order, simply move through your house in the opposite direction, starting out in the shower cubicle with the orange juice and finishing up by 'noticing' the six eggs on the hall table.

How to Succeed with Memory Test Four

One way in which the final test can be accomplished is by associating each number with a rhyming object. This is termed a 'peg-word system'.

A possible list of peg-word associations could be: 1 = bun; 2 = shoe; 3 = tree; 4 = door; 5 = hive; 6 = sticks; 7 = heaven (an angel); 8 = plate; 9 = wine; 10 = hen.

For 0, use the shape to remind you of a circus or wedding ring.

The test number 299,792.458 now becomes: a *shoe* (2), in which are two glasses of *wine* (99), with an *angel* (7) drinking a third glass of *wine* (9) while wearing a *shoe* (2). The angel is entering heaven through a *door* (4). As it swings open, you see a *hive* (5) and an ornamental *plate* (8).

Gather these images into a mind movie and you will be able to remember this number, which happens to be the speed of light in kilometres per second, at the speed of light!

If you deal with numbers frequently and have an excellent memory for them, such a technique may seem absurd and unnecessary. Yet associating numbers with images is one of the ways in which the Russian journalist Shereshevskii recalled complex mathematical equations. Here, for example, is part of his explanation of how he remembered the meaningless formula illustrated on page 75.

Neiman (N) came out and poked with his stick(.) He looked at a dried-up tree which reminded him of a root ($\sqrt{}$) and he thought: 'It's no wonder that this tree withered and that its roots were lain bare, seeing that it was already standing when I built these houses, these two here (d^2),' and again he poked with his stick(.). He said: 'The houses are old, a cross (x) should be placed on them.'

This gives a great return on his original capital, he invested 85,000 roubles in building them. The roof finishes off the building (—), and down below a man is standing and playing a harmonica (the x).[8]

However bizarre this anecdote may appear, it allowed Shereshevskii to recall the formula without a single error, fifteen years after he had first read it.

Armed with the memory aids described above, you would probably approach a similar challenge to the one made to you on page 85 with greater optimism. If you previously rated your chances of success as poor, the likelihood is that next time around you will be far more confident.

The fact is that, for all practical purposes, human memory can be regarded as limitless. It has been suggested, for example, that we could remember eleven new items per second from birth onwards into ripe old age, and still have plenty of storage space left.

Refuse to indulge in negative self-doubt about your powers of memory, since this merely makes one less confident and more anxious when faced with any challenge demanding reliable retention and recall.

At the same time, as I emphasized earlier, always bear in mind the Chinese saying: 'The palest ink is better than the best memory.'

Whenever possible, always make notes, keep records and develop effective systems for accessing your stores of knowledge. The less *inessential* information you keep in mind, the more certain can you be that you will be able to access what is *essential* more rapidly and accurately.

Finally, keep in mind the old physical fitness slogan, 'Use it or lose it', since it applies as much to memory as to muscles.

The harder you make your memory work in your life, and the greater your confidence in it, the more likely will it be that it will serve you faithfully throughout a good, long life.

SUMMARY

- Limit the amount of information you try to remember. Commit to memory only that information which is both relevant to your needs and valid.
- If memorizing it is going to be tough and/or time-consuming, always use some other form of storage whenever possible.
- Be wary of the accuracy of your recollections. As I explained, both in this chapter and in the discussion of 'confabulation' in Chapter Two, mistakes can easily be made even by those who, justifiably, take pride in their powers of memory. The greatest caution should be reserved for memories of fleeting events, especially those that were unexpected.
- Break large amounts of information into smaller and more manageable chunks.
- Rehearse information you need to learn at specific periods after first being exposed to it. Go over the key points in your mind at intervals of five minutes, one hour, three hours and six hours.

- Use bizarre mental images to remind you of key points. Link these together to create a 'mind movie'. Replaying that series of images will help you recall all the items easily and accurately.
- Develop a positive attitude towards your ability to retain and recall information accurately.
- The more you tell yourself (or others) what a shocking memory you have, the more likely it is that you will fulfil that gloomy prophecy.

6   Problem-Solving and Information Overload

'Hey, we've got a problem here!'
Astronaut Fred W. Haise

That laconic comment, broadcast around the world on 13 April 1970, announced a potentially fatal systems failure aboard the Apollo 13 moon mission. Their problem was that, 330,000 kilometres from Earth, the spacecraft had just blown up!

Only minutes after the three-man crew had signed off from a television broadcast, there was a loud bang as one of the two oxygen tanks in the rear service module exploded. Immediately, red warning lights glowed in the cockpit, indicating that life-support systems were starting to shut down. At the same moment, the craft began rocking and tumbling violently as gas vented from the remaining tank.

Thanks to some highly creative problem-solving against the clock, the crew survived. But their brush with disaster graphically illustrates what problems are all about.

They arise, in business as much as in outer space, in one of two situations: either there is a divergence between what was expected and what actually occurred, or there is a divergence between what we currently know and what we wish or need to know.

1. THERE IS A DIVERGENCE BETWEEN WHAT WAS EXPECTED AND WHAT ACTUALLY OCCURRED.

In the case of Apollo 13, the oxygen tank was not expected to explode, but it did. In business you might, for example:

- *expect* the unit costs of a new product to be £x but find that it turns out to be 10 per cent more expensive, so significantly eroding your margins
- *expect* an investment in IT (information technology) to increase productivity, only to find output remaining stagnant.

This definition forms the basis of such widely used business strategies as Planned Program Budget System (PPBS) and Management by Objectives (MBO). In both, one first establishes goals and then monitors differences between the current situation and the desired state of affairs.

Problems like this, which have more than one solution, are termed 'divergent'. Most of the problems we encounter in business fall into this category, and they often require a highly creative approach in order to come up with the best answer.

2. A DIVERGENCE BETWEEN WHAT YOU CURRENTLY KNOW AND WHAT YOU WISH OR NEED TO KNOW.

- You know your sales staff must make many calls each day in different towns, and you need to know the most efficient way they can travel between those calls.
- You know the overheads on your city-based HQ, and you need to know the savings made by moving out of town.

This type of problem, which usually has only one right answer, is termed 'convergent'.

Divergent problems are *usually* harder to solve than convergent problems, in which the answer can often be obtained by applying a standard formula or algorithm. I say *usually* because, although some convergent problems may appear simple at the outset, they are actually fiendishly difficult to solve and have engaged the brains of some of the world's finest mathematicians – the salesmen problem being a case in point.

Problems, therefore, result from various types of change:

- Changes we must make to go from what we know to what we need to know.
- Unanticipated changes that cause a deviation from a desired goal.
- Anticipated changes that fail to occur, so preventing a goal from being achieved.

- Changes that happen more rapidly or more slowly than expected.
- Changes that differ from those that were anticipated.
- Changes you wish or need to bring about in order to achieve a desired goal.
- Changes you wish or need to prevent occurring in order to achieve a desired goal.

As you can see, change is not only an intrinsic element of all problems, it also provides the means by which many solutions may be found, as the following example clearly illustrates.

THE SUBMARINE PROBLEM

In 1941, German submarines were causing havoc among Allied shipping. Every time they were spotted, there was a race between the submarine attempting to crash-dive to safety and the aircraft of RAF Coastal Command trying to sink it. The attacking aircraft dropped depth-charges set to detonate at thirty metres, the depth a submarine was expected to reach in the two minutes between their observing the plane and diving. Any submarine within about six metres of such an explosion would be destroyed, while those outside the lethal radius would suffer varying degrees of damage.

However logical this approach might appear, the events of 1941 soon revealed it to be a dangerous miscalculation, with 97 per cent of submarines surviving to fight again. British experts identified five possible changes that might provide a solution to this urgent problem:

- Improve the ability of the aircraft to spot the submarine.
- Make it harder for the submarine to spot the aircraft.
- Use faster aircraft.
- Increase the accuracy of the bombing.
- Change the depth at which the charges were set to explode.

Although all were viable and some were implemented, it was the final suggested change that made the greatest difference. This was proposed by a physicist, Dr E. J. Williams, who spotted a fallacy in the argument for setting depth charges to detonate at thirty metres. He pointed out that, while it might be true that, *on average*, submarine crews had sufficient warning to crash-dive to such a depth, once they had vanished below the waves it was impossible to bomb them with any accuracy, which meant that the majority was bound to escape serious damage. Those that failed to spot the attacking aircraft in time, however, also emerged unscathed, with depth-charges exploding harmlessly well below their keels.[1]

Dr Williams's easily implemented change was to set the charges so they exploded at a depth of eight metres. While this tactic enabled alert crews – the ones who could crash-dive to thirty metres in time – to escape, it made little difference to the success rate, since they were already likely to do so in any event. Less alert commanders who failed to reach a safe depth now paid a high price for their inattention. The number of confirmed 'kills' increased by a factor of four, leading German crews to believe that a new and far more powerful explosive had been introduced!

Half a century later, the way in which this practical solution to a deadly dangerous wartime problem was found still has important lessons to teach us today. While business problems are rarely so dramatic or life-threatening, the four-stage process used to resolve these situations works just as effectively if you are faced with finding answers against the pressures created by overload.

1 **Formulation** – clearly identifying the cause of the divergence.
2 **Interpretation** – what do we know about this divergence?
3 **Creation** – what can we do to fix the divergence?
4 **Implementation** – removing or reducing the divergence.

STAGE 1 - FORMULATION

As a teenager, my hobby was constructing a variety of electronic gadgets. These were relatively straightforward devices so, when a fault developed, finding out what had gone wrong was fairly easy. It usually came down to a dud component or dry solder.

Identifying problems on present-day electronic equipment, with scores of miniature components packed together on printed circuit board, is often so time-consuming that it is usually easier to junk and replace the entire board. It's the same with information overload. The more you know, or can know, about the reasons for a divergence, the harder it often is to find out why it is happening. As US President Grover Cleveland once remarked: 'It isn't that they can't see the solution. It is that they can't see the problem.'

This aspect of 'losing sight of the forest because of the trees' – a dilemma Lotus CEO Jim Manzis has described as 'getting lost in the bark' – makes it harder to identify exactly what the *real* problem is. As a result, we may come up with good answers to the wrong questions.

As an example, consider a software company for which I acted as a consultant a few years ago. They had set up a system for repairing television sets at low cost, by installing terminals in hundreds of small television repair shops. When given a set for repair, all the engineer had to do was log on to their system, carry out a series of diagnostic tests that appeared on-screen, and then replace the parts as instructed by the computer. The company's arrangement was to charge only for the time spent on line to their mainframe that carried out the diagnostics and identified the faulty component. The terminals were installed free of charge.

It seemed like a winning formula, and they sat back and waited for the money to pour in. The results were disappointing. Only a tiny proportion of TV service engineers logged on to the system, and revenue was, to say the least, sluggish. Deciding that their software must be insufficiently user-friendly, they invested further money having it rewritten. Still the uptake was too low. Next they decided to lower their on-line costs. It made little difference. The divergence between expected and actual revenues remained significant.

At my suggestion they took a different tack. What, I asked, was the reason why they believed TV service engineers (as opposed to their employers) should want to log on to the system?

'Because it makes the job of repairing televisions quick and easy,' came the response.

'How,' I asked, 'does this benefit the engineers, who may well regard such automatic repairs as a threat to their own job security?' After all, if a school-leaver with scarcely any knowledge or experience can now fix faulty sets, what's to stop employers sacking their highly trained and well-paid technicians and replacing them with a bunch of school-leavers?

What they needed to change was the benefit to the technician. Lower prices for the system appealed only to shop-owners, while making the interface even simpler to use merely increased the technician's sense of insecurity. The change I suggested involved turning the system into a lottery, with prizes awarded randomly, whenever a technician logged on to the system using his or her ID. The money spent on this promotion could be tightly regulated and the regular prizes were kept low, with one big monthly bonus prize. As a result, TV repair technicians virtually queued up to go on line! They even encouraged friends and neighbours to bring sets in for repair so as to enhance their chances of winning the jackpot.

When formulating a problem, ask yourself:

- What is *really* causing the divergence between the desired and the actual outcome?
- What is *not* causing the divergence?
- What is *distinctive* about this divergence?
- Where is the divergence occurring?
- Where *isn't* the divergence occurring?
- What is different about the situation in which the divergence occurs?
- When does the divergence occur?
- When *doesn't* the divergence occur?
- What's different or what has changed in the period when the divergence occurs?
- How important is the divergence?

Always put the divergence into perspective before spending time in looking for ways for preventing or reducing it.

Ask yourself whether there *really* is a problem, or is the goal(s) unreasonable or unrealistic? For example, is an expected production target too high ever to be achieved? If so, the divergence may be impossible to correct unless the goal, or the way of achieving it, is changed in some way.

One practical and easily implemented procedure for identifying the cause of a divergence is to create a Problem Understanding Box (PUB).

The PUB Approach

No matter how many possible causes there may be for a particular divergence, this structured procedure will always get to the root of any divergence. Here's an example of PUB in action.

Bismarck Manufacturing is looking to expand its business, but every attempt to increase production fails to meet the desired output target.

The managers know there are several possible reasons but cannot decide which is most likely to be producing the divergence. Their first task is to:

1. ASK A QUESTION

In Bismarck's case this is simply: 'Why can't our company expand?'

Once you have written down a clear and precise question, move to the second step and generate a list of possible causes.

2. LIST THE MOST LIKELY CAUSES OF THE DIVERGENCE

Bismarck managers now write down all the likely barriers to expansion. These include:

1. out-of-date equipment
2. too few staff
3. lack of clear goals
4. poor internal communications
5. insufficient advertising
6. inadequate computer systems.

Note that you should write down only possible causes that it is within your power to change. Those that are impossible to alter must be ignored.

Reviewing the list of possible changes, it is immediately apparent to Bismarck's management team that (1) out-of-date equipment overlaps with (6) inadequate computer systems. These two causes can, therefore, be combined into one: 'out-of-date equipment'.

When you have been through the whole list and have combined any similar causes, you can start creating the Problem Understanding Box.

3. CREATING THE PUB

Draw a rectangle and divide it into a grid which contains the same number of rows and columns (rows are horizontal, columns are vertical) as there are possible causes in your problem. In the Bismarck example, the grid would be five columns high and five rows wide, as illustrated below:

Next, identify each of the possible causes with a letter, such as A = out-of-date equipment; B = too few staff, and so on.

Now, label each row and column with each letter in order, as illustrated below:

The next step is to draw a cross in the squares that run diagonally from the top left corner to the bottom right corner (they are to be ignored) and write each problem next to its letter in each row:

	A	B	C	D	E
A. Out-of-date equipment	X				
B. Too few staff		X			
C. No clear goals			X		
D. Lack of communication				X	
E. Not enough advertising					X

Now you can start to make your judgements on the different causes.

4. JUDGING THE CAUSES

Consider each problem in turn and compare it to all the others.

The first empty box in row A is in line with column B. We call this box A:B since it is row A column B.

In this box, the Bismarck team compare cause A (out-of-date equipment) with cause B (too few staff). All they have to decide is: 'Which is more significant in producing the divergence?'

If they think that out-of-date equipment is more likely to be causing the problem than too few staff, they write a '1' in this A:B box. If they believe that lack of staff rather than outdated equipment is more important, they place a 'o' in this A:B box. For our example, we'll say the team consider outdated equipment to be more important than lack of staff, so they write a '1' in the A:B box.

Next, they go to the B:A box and write in a 'o'. This follows logically, since if A is a more important reason than B, then B must be less important than A. The Bismarck management grid now looks like this:

	A	B	C	D	E
A	✕	1			
B	o	✕			
C			✕		
D				✕	
E					✕

They repeat this task along row A, then continue with row B and so on, until the whole grid is filled in, as shown overleaf:

	A	B	C	D	E
A	X	1	1	1	1
B	0	X	1	0	0
C	0	0	X	1	0
D	0	1	0	X	1
E	0	1	1	0	X

5. CALCULATING THE IMPORTANCE OF CAUSES

All that remains for the Bismarck team to do is to total the number of 1's in each row, like this:

	A	B	C	D	E	
A	X	1	1	1	1	4
B	0	X	1	0	0	1
C	0	0	X	1	0	1
D	0	1	0	X	1	2
E	0	1	1	0	X	2

They now rewrite their list of possible causes according to these scores, placing the one with the highest total at the top of the list and the one with the lowest at the bottom.

Like Bismarck's managers, you will sometimes find causes that have the same totals. If this happens, you simply create a new mini-decision grid with only these causes included (see below).

	D	E
D	X	1
E	0	X

	B	C
B	X	1
C	0	X

In the Bismarck example, two pairs of causes have the same totals. Therefore, we have to create two mini-grids to decide which cause in each pair is more significant. As D and E have totals of 2 in the original grid, they are more significant than B and C. The above mini-grids tells Bismarck's managers that cause D is more significant than cause E and that cause B is more significant than cause C. Their order of significance now becomes:

A. out-of-date equipment
D. lack of communication
E. not enough advertising
B. too few staff
C. no clear goals.

6. FORMULATING THE KEY PROBLEM

Once all the possible causes for the divergence have been arranged in order in the way described above, and any causes with the same value have been ordered using a mini-grid, you can easily identify and formulate the key problem, since this is the one with the highest score.

By focusing your time and effort on this underlying cause, you will maximize your efforts towards finding a solution.

PUB is a powerful and easy-to-use technique which can be used to compare any number of potential causes – from two to two hundred!

Having formulated the cause of the divergence clearly, and having ensured you are actually dealing with the core issue rather than with less relevant or even with irrelevant matters, it is time to move to the second stage of problem-solving:

STAGE 2 - INTERPRETATION

This second stage of problem-solving also becomes harder when there are large amounts of information to consider. You are painfully aware that much of it must be irrelevant, but which of the myriad facts and figures at your disposal is mere distraction and which falls in the RR (Rolls-Royce) category by being both Relevant and Reliable?

Today, when more and more business solutions are based on the cycling and recycling of old information, there is an additional risk that certain ideas and assumptions are being taken for granted. They establish themselves so firmly in the minds of managers that their relevance and reliability are never questioned, let alone doubted. This may lead to overly elaborate solutions being proposed. This tendency towards complexity was first demonstrated some thirty years ago by Peter Wason of University College, London.[2] In an experiment, he showed people the numbers 2, 4 and 6, in that order, and explained that the sequence was determined by a simple rule which they must discover. To do this, they would offer what they believed were further examples of the rule in action, and he would tell them whether that sequence was right or wrong. From this feedback the participants would, when they were certain, tell him the rule. If, for example, the subject suspected that the rule was 'the number increases by two each time', they might suggest '1, 3, 5' or '3, 5, 7' as an example of the rule in action. (The rule was, in fact, merely that the numbers should increase in value; the way they did so was not relevant.) The majority of those taking part, however, jumped to the conclusion that it must be more complicated than this and they never looked for any evidence which could have disproved their assumption.[3]

The clear message is that we should always search for evidence that disconfirms our most cherished beliefs, especially when these cause needless complications. A convenient rule-of-thumb, devised by the fourteenth-century English philosopher William Ockham and known as 'Ockham's razor', cautions us that 'Entities should not be multiplied unnecessarily.' In other words, we should always use the most economical and least complex assumptions when formulating a problem.

Yet another barrier to distinguishing between relevant and irrelevant information erected by overload is an emotional one. When the problem appears impossible to solve within the time available, we can easily slip into one of the two mental states described in Chapter Five: defensive avoidance or hyper-vigilance.

During my lectures and workshops on information overload, I create these states of mind among my audience by asking them to test their IQ. If you would like to do so now, follow the instructions in the box below:

TEST YOUR IQ

All you need to do is note how long it takes you to come up with an answer to the following problem.

I like the colour red less than I like the colour blue.
But I prefer pink to yellow.
I don't like the colour orange as much as I like red.
But I think blue is less attractive than yellow.

Which of these five colours do I like the best?

Start the time now.

My answer is: (check this is correct with the answer below).

My time was:

WHAT YOUR RESULT REVEALS

	Time taken	IQ Score
Your IQ at a glance:	1–15 seconds	150 Genius level
	16–20 seconds	120 High
	21–30 seconds	100 Average
	31+	90 Below average
	Could not answer	60 Sub-Normal
	Failed to attempt it	
	Got the answer wrong	

How did you do and how do you feel about the result?

Delighted?

Indignant?

Dismissive?

If you hold that last opinion, you're right!

While your success or failure in solving the colour problem probably reveals something about your approach to this kind of mental challenge, it does **not** give an indication of IQ as I suggested

---

Answer: pink

above. That was a deliberate deception on my part to try to generate one of the two attitudes described above.

If you told yourself, 'I would sooner not know my IQ' or 'I'm just not interested in this type of challenge', you were taking refuge in defensive avoidance.

If you started to read the problem and became increasingly confused as the seconds ticked by, you were experiencing a mild state of hyper-vigilance.

The Building Blocks of Problem-Solving

In order to discover why a divergence has occurred, we must correctly identify and understand the three components which form the building blocks of every problem you will ever encounter, from the simplest to the most complicated. They are called the Givens, the Operations and the Goals, terms devised by Wayne Wickelgren, Professor of Psychology at the University of Oregon.[4] The Givens comprise everything we know, or can find out, about the problem. The Operations consist of what we can do with what we know. Goals comprise what we are seeking to achieve.

I shall deal with Operations and Goals later in this chapter. When interpreting information, what we must mainly focus on are the Givens. Identify these by asking yourself: What do I know, can I know or should I know, about this problem?

If uncertain about the reliability of some of your Givens, rate them on a scale of 1 to 5, where 5 = very reliable and 1 = very doubtful.

Recheck any Given with a rating of less than 4. Ask yourself: Have I explored all possible meanings and implications of the Givens? Have I been misled by false assumptions about the Givens? Are there other ways of looking at the Givens? Do I need further Givens before being able to arrive at an answer?

Let's apply this process to a problem.

HOW FAR DOES A FLY FLY?

Two cyclists are twenty kilometres apart on a long, straight track. At the same moment they start riding towards each other at a constant ten kilometres per hour. At the moment one of the cyclists starts to pedal, a fly on his handlebars takes off and flies to the second bicycle, then immediately returns to the first. The fly continues flying to and fro along the ever-decreasing distance as the cyclists approach each other. The fly's speed is recorded as forty-five kph. Assuming that no time is lost as the fly turns around at the bikes, how far will it have flown when the cyclists eventually meet?

There are two ways one might tackle this problem. One is by using some fairly complex mathematics, the other by applying a little common sense, coupled with a clear understanding of the Givens.

1. Two cyclists are on a straight track twenty kilometres apart.
2. They cycle towards one another at a constant speed of ten kph.
3. From this it is easy to deduce a third Given: that they will meet in one hour's time.
4. The fly's speed is forty-five kph.
5. In one hour, therefore, the fly will have travelled forty-five kilometres, and that is the required answer.

Now try your skill on a problem that has been around since at least 1911 and that is almost always answered incorrectly. Not only that, but many people refuse to accept the right answer, even when the logic behind the solution is pointed out to them!

A man studying a portrait says: 'Brothers and sisters have I none, but this man's father is my father's son!' Whose picture is he looking at?

The answer most frequently given is that he must be looking at a portrait of himself. But this is wrong. The mistake arises because the problem has been constructed in such a way to make the Givens hard to interpret.

Let's start by examining the clause: '. . . this man's father is my father's son!' Ask yourself what this means. If you are a male, who is your father's son? To put it another way, who is the son of your father? Since you have no brothers (first Given), you are your father's only son. So the Given here is really: 'I am this man's father.' In other words, he is looking at a picture of his own son.

With convergent problems, such as the two examples I have just provided, there is normally only one correct way to interpret the Givens. Make a mistake at this point and you will be almost certain to come up with the wrong answer.

In business, as I explained earlier, most problems are divergent ones and their Givens can have a number of possible – and sometimes equally valid – interpretations. One of the problems to which men and women are most likely to come up with very different answers is as follows. You have a four-legged table which wobbles. How would you set about making it stable? Think about this for a moment and see what answers you can come up with.

Possible solutions might be to wedge a small piece of folded paper under the shortest leg, or cut a piece off the other legs, or move the table to another part of the room if you suspect that the floor, rather than the table, is causing the problem. All could be perfectly valid answers.

How would you correct the same problem with a three-legged table? Again spend a moment thinking about it. If you came up with a similar set of solutions, you fell into a trap. The first problem is divergent and has a number of correct answers. The second is convergent, in that there is only one correct solution – three-legged tables cannot wobble!

In practice, one sex tends to spot this fallacy fairly frequently, while the other comes up with answers to a non-existent problem. I leave it to you to conduct some experiments and see whether it is men or women who are most likely to spot the trap.

Before trying to solve problems, always be sure that one exists in the first place. The most dangerous word in problem-solving is 'assume'. With that caution in mind, try your hand at this problem. A candle is fifteen centimetres long and its shadow is forty-five centimetres longer. How many times is the shadow longer than the candle? Think about this for a moment and try to come up with a solution.

When I have given this problem to large numbers of people attending my workshops to solve, a majority have said, 'Three times longer.' But this is wrong. Re-read the problem and, this time, notice that the candle's shadow is forty-five centimetres *longer* than the candle. In other words the shadow is sixty centimetres in length and, therefore, *four* times as long as the candle.

If you got it wrong, it was through making a faulty assumption about the length of the shadow. But don't feel bad about that. It's a mistake made by around 90 per cent of those who are presented with the challenge. Try it for yourself and see how many of your friends and colleagues also fall into the assumption trap.

You'll find that, in the words of the nineteenth-century American humorist, Josh Billings: 'The trouble with people is not so much that they don't know but that they know so much that ain't so.'[5]

STAGE 3 – CREATION

At this stage of problem-solving, one is mainly exploring what Operations are necessary to correct the divergence and achieve the desired Goal. They are the means by which you can travel from where you are now, to where you want to be.

As explained above, with convergent problems, the Operations may be stated in a straightforward manner as a formula or algorithm; this tells you exactly how to proceed from where you are to where you want to be, with each intermediate step clearly identified and spelt out.

Divergent problems have not only a wider range of Givens, but also many more possible Operations. Because this stage of problem-solving is so vital, I have devoted the whole of the next chapter to it.

STAGE 4 – IMPLEMENTING THE SOLUTION

In the pressure cooker of modern business, there is an increasing temptation to go for 'quick fixes' rather than more visionary, longer-term solutions. Managers overloaded with information are at a greater risk of succumbing to this temptation, since the uncertainty created by a mismatch inevitably arouses a degree of anxiety. The more serious the problem and the less time there is in which to come up with a solution, the greater this anxiety is likely to prove. The moment a solution is found, the problem-solver is 'rewarded' by the removal of that distressing uncertainty.

There is often a tremendous sense of relief at 'putting the problem behind you' and moving on to the next challenge, even if at the back of your mind you are uncomfortably aware that the chosen solution may offer only a short-term answer.

Where the Goal itself is uncertain or is imprecisely stated, the risk of an inappropriate solution being implemented becomes all the greater. In my experience, the truly successful leaders of organizations have one thing in common: a very clear sense of direction. They are pragmatic visionaries, prepared to sacrifice short-term gains provided the prospect of longer-term profits are sufficiently attractive.

This sense of direction enables them to define and state tough but realistic Goals in a way that inspires their followers to even greater efforts. Weak and ineffectual CEOs, by contract, set no clear course, have shifting goals and often change course in mid-voyage. The result is confusion, wasted effort and loss of morale among those slaving away below decks. As the Roman philosopher Lucius Seneca wisely pointed out: 'For the ship without a harbour, no wind ever blows in the right direction.'

The importance of clearly understanding your Goal when faced with a problem is well illustrated by the following example.

The Horserace

A wealthy merchant had two sons, each of whom owned a fine stallion; the young men argued continually over whose mount was the faster. Tired of this bickering, their father offered them a wager. His entire fortune, he said, would go to the son whose steed arrived *last* in the main square of a town some distance away. Eagerly the young men mounted up and started to ride as slowly as possible towards the town. A week later they had travelled only a short distance from their father's home and it seemed that the 'race' would continue until the animals died of old age. Fortunately for them, and for this problem, a wise man passed by and gave them some advice. Seconds later, the two boys were racing hell for leather towards the distant town.

What was the sage's advice?

If you are unable to find the answer, it is almost certainly because you have incorrectly understood the Goal. What their father said was that his fortune would go to the son whose *horse* reached the town square last, not to the *son* who arrived last. To achieve this Goal, all they needed to do was to exchange horses! The son who won the race would then be on his brother's mount, which meant that his own steed arrived last. It is the same in business and in our personal life. Many people fail to solve problems because they do not properly understand their Goal(s).

An ambitious female executive once complained to me that she found it difficult to assert herself with male subordinates. She assumed that her

Goal was merely to become more assertive. But she was wrong. Her true Goal was to find a way of asserting herself while still being regarded as a 'nice' person.

Ask yourself: Am I clear about my Goal(s)? Is the Goal believable and achievable? Are there other possible Goal(s) that would be equally satisfactory? Have I explored the selected Goal(s) from all angles? Are emotions adversely affecting my judgement of the desirability or otherwise of my Goal(s)? Is there an element of wishful thinking in this choice of Goal(s)? How will I know when the Goal(s) has/have been achieved? This can happen only if there is some way of quantifying outcome; for instance, if your goal is to increase productivity in your company, what criteria will you be using to measure that increase?

If you are unable to see how a desired Goal can be attained, consider whether the Goal might be viewed in some other way. Think in terms of opposites and you will often spot what needs to be done in order to reach a solution. If, for example, your Goal was to *raise* something, and this appears impossible, consider whether the Goal might not also be achieved by *lowering something else*. If the Goal is to make something come *first* and you can see no way by which such an outcome could be managed, ask yourself whether, by making something else come *last*, you might not achieve the same result.

In their business classic *The Goal*, Eli Goldratt and Jeff Cox[6] provide an excellent example of this kind of lateral thinking. The hero, Alex Rogo, is a harassed factory manager, working with increasing desperation to improve output as his company heads rapidly for disaster. Beset by problems in his private life, the last straw is having to lead a group of Boy Scouts on a lengthy hike. However, it is while trying to achieve the goal of getting his youthful troop to their destination on time that he stumbles on the answer to his business problems. Because the boys walk at different speeds, the line is soon widely spaced out and, collectively, they are covering only two kilometres an hour rather than the required four. Slowest of all is Herbie, a boy weighed down by an enormous backpack.

Alex realizes that the real goal of the hike is for all the Scouts to arrive at their destination as a unit, rather than as individuals with varying levels of fitness. To achieve this new goal, he arranges them with the fastest, fittest boys at the rear of the line and Herbie leading the way. When the faster boys grumble, he explains the goal is '. . . not to see who can get there the fastest. The idea is to get there together. We're not a bunch of individuals out there. We're a team.'

Before long, however, the faster boys are complaining even more bitterly about the pace. So he suggests that they share Herbie's burden by distributing some of the heavy items from his backpack among the entire troop. 'Again, we start walking. But this time, Herbie really can move. Relieved of most of the weight of his pack, it's as if he's walking on air. We're flying now, doing twice the speed as a troop that we did before. And we still stay together. Inventory is down. Throughput is up.'

Alex Rogo solved the problem of the troop and saved his factory by re-stating the Goal and approaching it from an entirely different direction.

Having clearly stated what it is you want to achieve, the final stage is to implement the Operations by which the divergence between the present and the desired outcome can be attained. This stage too is adversely affected by overload. The more that is known, or can be known, about the possible consequences of an outcome, the more conservative many individuals, and organizations, become. Overload can more easily lead to the creation of what I term a 'Yes but . . .' culture, in which nervous managers come up with reasons for not implementing a suggested solution.

The more we know, the easier it becomes to find contrary arguments and opposing viewpoints, and so we can quickly reach a situation in which, in the worlds of Hamlet:

> '. . . the native hue of resolution
> Is sicklied o'er with the pale cast of thought,
> And enterprises of great pith and moment,
> With this regard, their currents turn awry
> And lose the name of action.'

This too can become more difficult under information overload, especially when the proposals are controversial or their outcomes are less than certain.

Opponents, whether or not justified in their opposition, find it easier to cite contrary evidence in support of their objections if large quantities of information on the topic are available. Using their counter arguments, they may slow or even put a complete halt to the solution's implementation. A good example is the current search for solutions to the threat of global warming. No sooner have scientists come up with proposals to eliminate one of the causes than pressure groups produce evidence that casts doubts on those suggestions. This is not to say they are right or wrong to do so, but merely to point out that, the more information there is, the harder it can be to implement a solution.

Implementing difficult or controversial solutions is never easy, especially when the underlying issues themselves are complex. As one CEO ruthfully commented to me: 'If the other side has an argument which is simple but wrong and you have one which is complicated but right, they're going to win.'

To turn answers into action often demands considerable social skill and the ability to communicate clearly and confidently. It is these talents above all that will help you to push through unpopular but unavoidable solutions.

In a study of 2,000 managers, Richard Boyatzis, a Boston management consultation firm, found that the style which effective executives adopted when working with others (i.e. how soft or tough they were) was less important to their success than their self-confidence, their skill at influencing others and their overall drive for excellence. To accomplish these goals, they also showed superior skill in taking advantage of opportunities and seizing every chance to display their abilities. The most successful implementers are those managers who are 'always strategizing'. Translated into the language of this book, they are always seeking ways of operating on their Givens in such a way as to achieve desired Goals.

Nothing I have written in this chapter should be taken to imply that I believe that solutions based on guesswork, hunches or ignorance are in any way superior to those founded on a careful, rational and objective identification and interpretation of relevant and reliable information. All I am saying is that overload makes it harder to decide why a divergence has occurred and how best that mismatch can be removed or reduced.

Fortunately, there are practical procedures for overcoming this obstacle. In Chapter Seven, I shall describe ways of analysing large quantities of information speedily and efficiently, even when working under the pressure of imminent deadlines.

SUMMARY

- Problems arise either when there is a divergence between what you expect to happen and what actually occurs, or when you cannot see how to get from a current state of knowledge to a new understanding.
- Convergent problems have just one correct answer. Divergent problems have a number of equally valid answers, although some will usually be superior to the rest.
- The most effective way to start your search for solutions to complex problems is by asking: What can I change?
- Having identified what *can* be changed, your next question should be: What effect will this change produce?
- There are four stages in solving a problem: Formulation, Interpretation, Creation and Implementation. Overload can adversely affect our ability to carry out any of these stages efficiently.
- To solve problems you must clearly understand their Givens, Operations and Goals.
- In business, successful problem-solvers always have clear Goals in mind. Ineffective ones typically have no clear idea where they or their companies should be going.

7

Creative Carving and Solution Trees

'The uncreative mind can spot wrong answers, but it takes a very creative mind to spot wrong questions.'

Antony Jay

When Walter Percy Chrysler was a young engineer, he saved for months to buy the latest motor car with the most advanced engineering available. Having driven his pride and joy just once, he took it into the workshop and dismantled it, nut by nut and part by part, until the result of months of scrimping and saving lay in pieces around him. Chrysler had bought the best car on the market just so that he could build an even better one. Taking it apart, or 'reverse engineering' it as we call it these days, was the only way by which he could find out how it had been put together.

Tackling problems by reverse engineering is not only a good deal cheaper and easier, it's also one of the fastest routes to finding the best solutions. You can see how the various elements within the problem interact with one another, you can identify key components and obtain a clear understanding of functional relationships. Dismantling must, of course, be performed carefully and methodically to avoid being left with a multitude of pieces and no idea how to put them back together again. Without a logical system of analysis, you are likely to produce more questions than answers and will end up in an even greater state of confusion. In this chapter, I shall be providing you with techniques for cutting problems down to size, in order to decide which Operations need to be performed on the Givens in order to achieve a desired Goal. The basic questions you need to answer when searching for effective Operations are: What can I do with what I know? What methods can be used to move around the information provided by the Givens?

Here's a simple example of what I mean. Eight diplomats attend a conference. Each shakes hands with all the others just once. How many handshakes are there?

The most frequently given answer is 56 (i.e. 7×8).

If this is the answer you came up with, an error has occurred in your choice of the Operation chosen to manipulate the Givens, that is the eight diplomats. The correct solution is 28, and for this reason: once diplomat A has shaken hands with diplomat B, B has also shaken hands with A and does not need to do so again!

The failure to spot an obvious Operation is illustrated perfectly by the story of a motorist whose car got a puncture outside a mental hospital. He undid the four nuts that held the wheel in place and removed the flat tyre. Just as he was about to fit the new wheel back in place, he accidentally kicked the nuts and they disappeared down a drain. The motorist was staring in dismay at a wheel that he was now incapable of fixing to his car, when a patient from the hospital who had been watching offered a suggestion. 'Why not take a nut from each of your other wheels?' he said. 'The car will run perfectly safely with three nuts still holding each wheel, and you can drive to a garage and replace them.'

'What a brilliant idea,' the delighted motorist said. 'But how could I fail to see such an obvious solution when you, a madman, did so?'

'I'm insane,' the patient replied indignantly, 'not stupid!'

Not spotting an obvious Operation is frustrating and embarrassing, but we shouldn't feel too bad about such lapses. Research going back more than fifty years shows them to be an almost unavoidable aspect of normal thinking. Dr Karl Duncker, an early pioneer of problem-solving studies, used the term 'functional fixedness' to describe this creative blind spot.[1] In a typical experiment he would give subjects a candle, some matches, a matchbox and a thumb tack, then ask them to find a way of attaching the candle to a wooden post. In one version of his experiment, the four items were laid out separately on the table. In another, the matches were left inside the box. In the first experiment, few people failed to work out how the problem should be solved: they removed the drawer from the box, attached this to the post with the thumb tack, and then melted a little wax into the drawer to fix the candle securely in place.

When the box was presented to them full of matches, however, only a minority were able to recognize its second possible function as a candle-holder. They were blinded to this essential Operation by seeing the box *only* in its original role as something that held matches. In this case, their mindset prevented the subjects from seeing anything other than what they expected to see.

Here's a problem that the majority of people are unable to solve. Simply take a sheet of plain paper, or card, and reproduce the illustration shown below in Figure 7.1.

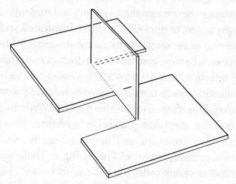

Figure 7.1 *'Reproduce this illustration with a piece of paper'*

It may appear straightforward; in fact, it can be solved only by abandoning an assumption that most people make about the nature of the illustration. I will give you the answer later in this chapter.

MINDSET AND MENTAL BLINDNESS

A tragic example of mental blindness – and one which led to the needless and agonizing deaths of hundreds of thousands of hospital patients – was the early discovery, and rejection, of bacterial infection. Nineteenth-century hospitals were unhealthy places in which to give birth. At the time, infections were believed to be caused by foul air – the word 'influenza', from the Italian for influence, is a legacy of that medical Given.

When women died, as thousands did, of puerperal fever, this too was blamed on contagion, a cause which was so widely accepted that, with only a few exceptions, no doctor challenged the view.

Around 1847, an observant Hungarian physician named Ignaz Semmelweiss disagreed. The chief doctor on the obstetric wards at Vienna's Allgemeines Krankenhaus, he had noticed that on the wards where medical students trained, deaths due to puerperal fever were around 18 per cent compared to just 3 per cent on those wards staffed only by midwives. Like any good scientist, Semmelweiss wanted to know why, and it was not long before the answer came to him. On wards where the death rate among mothers was highest, doctors and students came directly from the autopsy room, their clothes and hands smeared with blood and pus. Midwives and their teachers, by contrast, came from the lecture rooms. Semmelweiss became convinced that doctors and medical students were carrying infection into the wards. His answer was to insist that all the staff and students wash their hands with soap and water and soak them in chlorinated lime before examining patients. When this instruction was put into practice, mortality quickly declined from 18 to 1 per cent.

Was Semmelweiss promoted and honoured for his life-saving discovery? He most certainly was not! For daring to challenge the deeply entrenched mindset of his colleagues, the unfortunate Hungarian was demoted and his practising privileges limited. He presented a paper on the subject to the Medical Society of Vienna, but it was virulently attacked and he returned to Budapest. Broken by the hostility and indifference of his colleagues, he went insane and was sent to an asylum, where in 1865 he died, ironically of a blood infection.

Decades later, when Joseph Lister (1827–1912) rediscovered antisepsis, his views too were greeted with disbelief and hostility. Samuel Gross (1805–84), a leading American surgeon, wrote: 'Little if any faith is placed by any enlightened or experienced surgeon . . . in the so-called carbolic acid treatment of Professor Lister.'

But it's not just in the older disciplines such as medicine that mental blindness can strike. In 1943, IBM founder Thomas Watson commented: 'I think maybe there is a world market for maybe five computers.' Even Bill Gates, co-founder of Microsoft, espoused the view in 1981 that '640 kilobytes of memory ought to be enough for anybody'.

How To Be a Mind-Reader

You can demonstrate the effects of mindset for yourself by trying this simple experiment on friends and colleagues; it should give you a reputation as a mind-reader!

Ask them to pick a number between 1 and 9. Now they must multiply the number chosen by 9. If they have a two-digit number as a result of that multiplication (as they probably will have), tell them to add those two digits together. Next, tell them to subtract 5. The number that remains will determine a letter of the alphabet that they must now select. If, for example, if they were left with a 1, the letter would be A; 2 = B, 3 = C, and so on. Next, ask them to choose a country which starts with that letter of the alphabet. Now ask them to pick an animal that starts with the *second* letter of the country's name. Finally, they are to recall the colour of that animal.

Before conducting this experiment, write on a piece of paper: 'You are thinking of a grey elephant in Denmark.' On around 80 per cent of occasions you will, to their amazement, be proved absolutely right. 'How did you do it?' they will want to know. 'Are you a mind-reader?' The answer is far simpler, although I suggest you let them work it out for themselves. You have just taken advantage of their mindset.

Here's how it works. Any number between 1 and 9 which is multiplied by 9, has its two digits added together to produce a single number and then has 5 subtracted from that number will produce 4.

For example: Think of 3 ($3 \times 9 = 27$: $2 + 7 = 9$: $9-5 = 4$), or

$$9 \ (9 \times 9 = 81: 8 + 1 = 9: 9-5 = 4), \text{ or}$$
$$5 \ (5 \times 9 = 45: 4 + 5 = 9: 9-5 = 4).$$

The fourth letter of the alphabet is, of course, d. When asked to find a country which starts with d, the one most easily called to mind is Denmark. When asked to find an animal whose name starts with an 'e', the most common answer is elephant, which, of course, is grey.

Mindset is associated with another form of mental blindness, known as 'functional fixedness'. This means seeing, say, a paper clip only as a spoon rather than as an object that might be used in a variety of ways. Executives attending creativity courses are sometimes given an exercise designed to help them to recognize and defeat functional fixedness. They will be given an everyday object, let's say a paper clip, and asked to find as many uses for it as possible. I believe the world record is currently held by American Express executives, who dreamed up 1,000 uses for a paper clip. These included such suggestions as 'form it into a loop, add a drop of water and transform it into a magnifying glass' and 'use it with a thumb tack to produce a primitive but functional electric switch'.

As with Givens, in the real world, Operations tend to be almost as diverse as the imagination one brings to bear on a problem. One company was asked to design a compact jack which had to be contained in a box measuring no more than ten centimetres on one side but which should crank out to one metre and support a weight of up to four tonnes. During a brainstorming session in search of the necessary Operation to achieve this Goal, they compared what they were being asked to do with the Indian rope trick, in which a flexible rope magically becomes rigid. This creative imagery resulted in the Operation which led to a solution: two chains, each flexible in one direction, like bicycle chains, were forced together as they unrolled from the box, forming a single, rigid column.

Before arriving at any solution to a problem, therefore, answer the following questions. Have I identified the Operations correctly? Have I explored *all* the ways Givens can be operated upon, or only the more obvious ones?

The card problem I posed earlier in this chapter is an excellent example of the above trap. The assumption people often make is that they are looking at the *same surface* of the card on either side of the flap. If it is cut and folded, as shown opposite (Figure 7.2), you can easily reproduce the illustration.

Two powerful methods for solving the divergent problems which face people in business are Creative Carving and Solution Trees. The first technique enables you to slice complex problems into smaller, more manageable units, while the second lets you put them back together again.

USING CREATIVE CARVING

This technique was developed by George Miller, Professor of Psychology at Princeton University.[2] It is based on the eminently sensible, if rarely appreciated, notion that small, simple problems are easier to solve than big, complex ones.

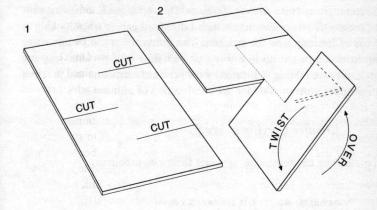

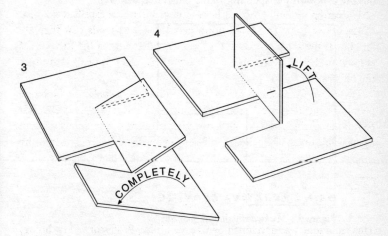

Figure 7.2

Creative carving enables you to reduce the available information to its key elements in a way that preserves the functional relationship between the various aspects of the task, and so allows the separated elements to be reconstructed into an overall answer. This technique is somewhat akin to progressive fragmentation, which I discussed earlier when looking at ways of learning new information. The difference is that, while study material can be cut up in a way that best suits your personal learning style, creative carving is dictated by the problem's structure and the need to produce units suitable for the construction of solution trees.

Creative Carving at Work

To illustrate this technique, consider these two problems.

PROBLEM NO. 1: THE L-SHAPED ROOM

Imagine you are the manager of a company that has just moved into new premises. Unfortunately, the only office available in the right location has the awkwardly shaped floor area illustrated below.

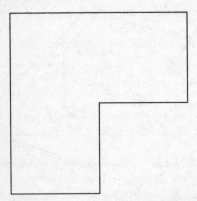

Figure 7.3 *'Awkwardly shaped floor area'*

Your problem is to divide this space into four identical offices for executives who have equal status within the company. In order to avoid morale-damaging friction, every office must be exactly the same size and shape. To add to your difficulties, you must use straight partitions; furthermore, each office will be fitted out with standard furnishings, so you must avoid producing oddly shaped rooms. You are under pressure to come up with a design: the builders are waiting on site to be told how to proceed, and any delay will waste money. Finally, your difficulties are compounded by the fact that you have forgotten to bring along a ruler or any other measuring device to help you calculate the floor area.

How quickly and easily can you solve the problem and achieve the Goal of designing four identical rooms in the space available?

PROBLEM NO. 2: LANGUAGE TEXTBOOKS

Imagine that you are the head of a school with 1,000 students. They are allowed to study either languages or a science subject.

At the start of the year you must order your textbooks. The head of the language department tells you that 400 students will be studying Spanish and 300 French. One hundred and fifty students want to study both Spanish and French. How many *science* textbooks must you order to ensure that each student *not* opting to study languages will have one?

Before we move on to see how effectively creative carving handles these problems, why not have a go at them, using whatever methods you would normally bring to bear on such challenges.

Now let's turn creative carving loose on the problems.

SOLUTION NO. 1: THE L-SHAPED ROOM

Your first thought when confronted by this problem may have been that the room can be divided only into *three* equal-sized offices, as shown in Figure 7.4 overleaf.

Perhaps you sketched in some partitions before realizing that this Operation will not achieve the desired Goal. If you did this, you were starting to creatively carve up the problem, but without any clear direction towards the final Goal. Had you continued to carve the problem in this way, however, the answer should quickly have become obvious (Figure 7.5 overleaf).

As this illustration shows, we have produced four equal-sized, identically shaped offices, as the problem demanded.

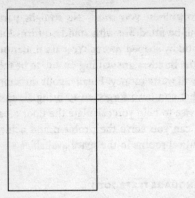

Figure 7.4 '. . . Divided into 3 equal-sized offices'

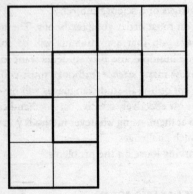

Figure 7.5 ". . . Divided into 4 equal-sized offices'

SOLUTION NO. 2: LANGUAGE TEXTBOOKS

The answer most frequently given to this problem is: 300 science textbooks will be needed. In fact this solution underestimates the demand by 150. To see why this is so, let's start by examining the Givens:

Total number of students	1,000
Students taking Spanish	400
Students taking French	300
Students taking both Spanish and French	150

The mistake made by people who give 300 as the answer is that they only consider the first three Givens and assume that 1,000 − (300 + 400) must mean that 300 students will be taking science. This assumes that the 150 students taking both languages are included in the larger numbers. This problem can be creatively carved by considering all three elements and the relationship between them. This is far easier to do by sketching the elements out as shown below.

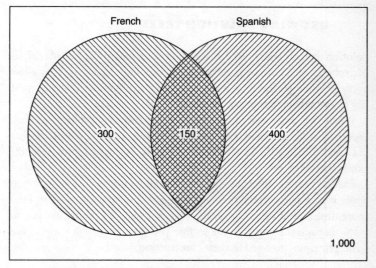

Figure 7.6 *'The rectangles and circles'*

In this illustration, the rectangle represents the total number of students in the school; the circle on the right shows the number of students taking Spanish and that on the left those taking French. The overlap between the circles indicates the 150 pupils studying both languages. Since these 150 students come into *both* groups, this number has to be taken away from the total in order to discover the total number studying languages.

We start by adding the students taking French (300) and Spanish (400) = 700

Then we subtract the number of students studying both: 700 − 150 = 550

Finally we subtract this total from 1,000, to find out how many students will be taking science rather than languages: 1,000 − 550 = 450. So 450 science textbooks must be ordered to ensure that each student taking this subject has the course text.

You will find that illustrating a problem in some way often aids your understanding of the Givens and safeguards you against any traps.

Having chopped a complicated problem down to size, the next stage is to rebuild it using the second of the two techniques I mentioned.

GROWING SOLUTION TREES

Solution trees are widely used by scientists when making a detailed analysis of problems that have to be solved using computer programs. They allow every possible pathway to a solution to be explored so that the most direct and reliable route can be found.

When the same approach is adopted for everyday problem-solving, especially in the face of overload, confusion is reduced; the speed, consistency and success with which effective Operations can be found is significantly increased.

For the purpose of explaining the procedure, however, I am going to apply it to a fairly straightforward problem that you will solve in little more time than it takes to read the Givens. Even so, I should like you to work through the tree with me so that you get a thorough grasp of the basic principles involved in their construction.

Water in the Desert

At a desert oasis you have the task of transferring exactly two litres of water from a full five-litre container into a ten-litre drum. The only other container is an empty three-litre drum. Because water is so precious, you cannot risk wasting a drop, and since working under the blistering sun is so exhausting you must not expend more energy than is absolutely necessary. What is the quickest and easiest method for making the transfer?

In a problem of this simplicity, many people would have no difficulty developing the required operation and then using it to mentally manipulate the Givens in order to achieve the desired Goal. Here we will create a solution tree to find the answer.

When developing any tree, the starting point is always to state the problem. When this is done, it is immediately clear that there are only two possible operations. Water can be poured from the five-litre can into either the three- or the ten-litre drum.

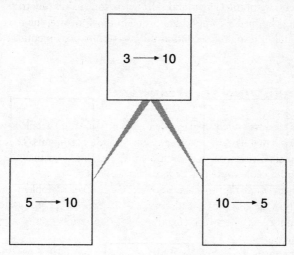

Figure 7.7 '*Water can be poured from the 5-litre can . . .*'

At this stage of the tree's growth, there are three possible ways of proceeding.

1. Water remaining in the five-litre container can be poured into the ten-litre drum.
2. Water in the three-litre container can be poured into the ten-litre drum.
3. Water in the ten-litre container can be poured into the three-litre drum.

These three options are now sketched into the developing tree (Figure 7.8, overleaf).

Clearly only the first and last moves will lead to the required Goal of leaving just two litres in the ten-litre container.

Operation Two fails to produce this result. We can easily show that this is a false move by writing out the tree to its final stage (Figure 7.9, p. 129).

In neither case do we finish up with the required Goal of leaving exactly two litres of water in the ten-litre drum.

The completed solution tree for this problem is shown on page 130.

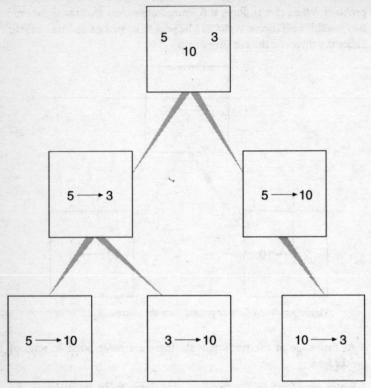

Figure 7.8 '*3 water options in a tree*'

All the problems we have explored so far are examples of convergent tasks. In each case there was only one *correct* solution, which was clearly specified in the problem statement. This does not mean, however, that there was only one Operation which would take you to the correct answer.

In the water problem it does not matter whether you started by pouring water from the five-litre drum into the three-litre or ten-litre drum, since this still leads to the required Goal.

Of these alternatives, the second (5 into 10) was slightly better in that it led clearly to the final answer, while the first Operation gave rise to the possibility, however slight, of pouring from the three-litre into the ten-litre drum and coming up with an incorrect answer.

With many problems, especially those for which you have a very large

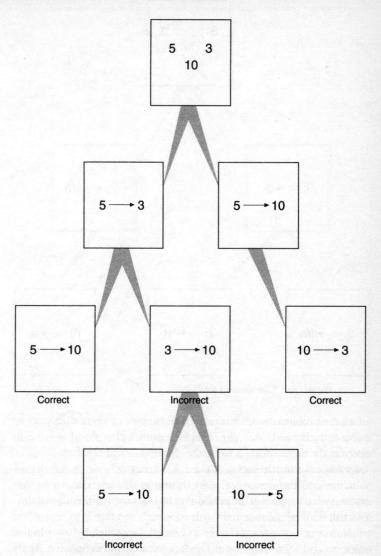

Figure 7.9 *'The final stage of the tree'*

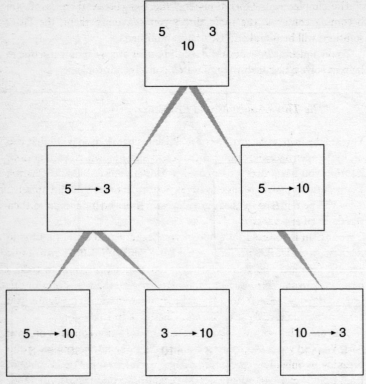

Figure 7.10 *'The solution tree'*

amount of information, there will be a number of alternative ways to arrive at the desired Goal. The skill of the proficient problem-solver is to discover the route which is most straightforward and risk-free.

In science and mathematics there is a constant striving for elegant solutions and theories. An elegant theory, in this context, is one that explains what happens in the most direct and economical manner possible. When developing solution trees to develop pathways through the problem which will take you from Givens to Goal(s), be guided by this ideal of economy and try to make your Operations as simple as possible. Apply Ockham's razor, as suggested in Chapter Six, and keep in mind Einstein's exhortation that 'everything in life should be made as simple as possible, but no simpler!'

The simpler your Operations are, the less chance there is of you becoming confused; the more direct you can make them, the faster solutions will be found and Goals accomplished.

To demonstrate how powerful solution trees are, we'll now use one to help us solve a reasonably complicated convergent problem.

The Three Salespersons Problem

You are the owner of a grocery store. Business has been so good that you decide to open a second branch on the other side of town. At your current location you have three experienced sales staff: Alice, Bill and Charles. You want to transfer all three to the new store in order to build up sales. They will be replaced by three novices, who must be trained up to their standards of excellence.

Your plan is to bring only one of your experienced staff at a time to the new store, work with him or her for a while until the new routine becomes familiar and then return to your original premises to train a new salesperson. You intend to alternate between the two stores in this way, until your original store is staffed by three new employees and you are working alongside Alice, Bill and Charles at the new store.

This would be a simple matter, were it not for some concerns on your part. You feel you are capable of training only one novice employee and breaking in only one experienced salesperson at a time. You also know, from bitter experience, that when Alice and Bill work unsupervised they soon start to argue, creating a disagreeable atmosphere in the store which upsets customers. You have also found it is a bad idea to leave Bill and Charles unsupervised because, being close friends, they waste time chatting.

In the past, none of these personality problems were important since you were always around to keep an eye on things. Now, since you want to transfer them to the new store one at a time, a situation could easily arise in which either Alice and Bill or Bill and Charles have to work together unsupervised. The original store is too small for more than five people to work in it at any one time, so you cannot hope to resolve your dilemma by increasing the number of staff.

Your challenge is to devise an Operation that satisfies these two conditions:

1. Novice sales staff must be trained and experienced staff familiarized with the new store. This has to be done in such a way that you finish up with your original premises staffed by the three newcomers, while you work with Alice, Bill and Charles in the new store.

2. At no time during the transitional period, however, can either Alice and Bill or Bill and Charles be left working together unsupervised.

In constructing the solution tree that will provide us with an Operation which solves this problem, the Givens – Alice, Bill and Charles – will be represented by A, B and C. The new salesperson will be X and you, the owner, will be U. The additional Givens, the old and new stores, will be depicted by boxes drawn in at each level of the tree's development. In computer-speak, the name used for such boxes is 'nodes', and this is the term I will be using from now on.

The root from which our tree will grow is shown below. From this starting point, try to work out a logical development for its growth before reading on.

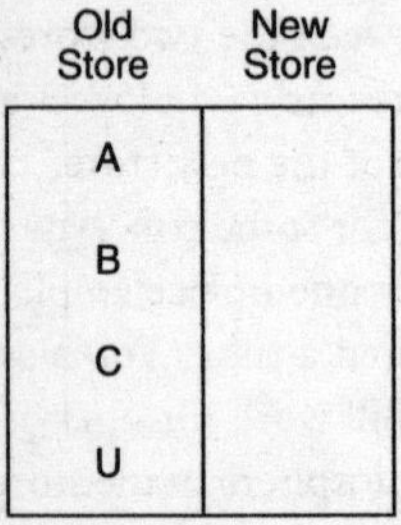

Old Store	New Store
A	
B	
C	
U	

Figure 7.11 *'ABC tree'*

How did you get on? Hopefully you found it fairly easy to put this invaluable problem-solving procedure to work. But if your tree seemed to lose its way after only modest growth had occurred, please don't feel discouraged or convince yourself that it is too complicated to bother with. Like any new skill, it takes time and practice to master. After only a few attempts, however, you should find the procedure flows smoothly, removing uncertainty and – no matter how complex or numerous the Givens – taking you directly to the required Goal.

Developing the Three Salespersons Solution Tree

Start by ensuring that your opening statement, the root from which your tree will be grown, satisfies the conditions in the problem.

Next consider all possible moves and write them out in full to produce the first level of the tree.

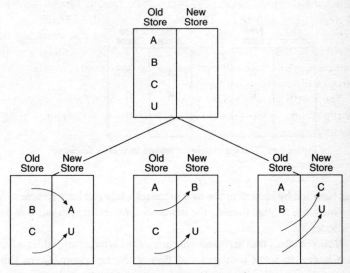

Figure 7.12 *'The three salespersons solution tree'*

Two of these Operations can be dropped straight away, because they violate conditions laid down by the problem. In (i), old friends Bill and Charles, left unsupervised together in the old store, will waste their time chatting. In (iii), Alice and Bill, without you being there to keep an eye on them, will sour the atmosphere by bickering. This leaves only the middle node (ii) to be developed further (Figure 7.13 overleaf).

We know from the problem statement that, having taken an experienced salesperson into your new store, you intend working there yourself until things are running smoothly. At this point you will return to the old store and train up a novice.

To create the next level of nodes, therefore, we will assume that Bill

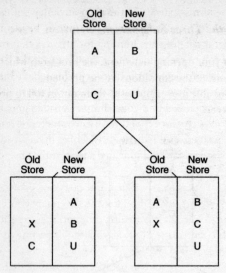

Figure 7.13 *'This leaves only the middle node to be developed further . . .'*

has been left by himself in the new premises while you have returned to the old store to start training the newcomer, represented in our tree by the letter X.

Now you must transfer a second experienced salesperson, either Alice or Charles, to work with you and Bob at the new store. Given this condition, you will see that the tree can now grow in only two ways. Node (i) illustrates the result of taking Alice along with you to the new premises, while (ii) shows what would happen if Charles were selected.

Note the X in the 'old store' to indicate that a novice salesperson has been installed. Studying this further growth in the solution tree, we find that both combinations violate a condition set down in the problem. If you take Alice with you (node (i)), then Bill and Alice will be left alone together in the new store when you return to the old store to train the newcomer. Similarly, if you decide to take Charles along with you (node (ii)), then he will be working unsupervised with Bill after your departure, another combination that needs to be avoided. Does this mean your problem has no solution?

There certainly are complex real-life problems for which no solutions exist, at least not in the terms stated, and the great advantage of using a solution tree is that such intractable challenges can quickly be identified. This will save you a great deal of time hunting for answers that do not exist. They also enable you to reconsider either the Givens or the Goal(s) so as to reformulate the problem, if possible in terms which make it capable of resolution. A problem of this sort, however, is most unlikely not to yield an answer. When you find yourself up against an apparently insoluble outcome, it pays to suspect you have encountered a trap. As with many real-world business problems, the answer lies in reconsidering the information provided and taking a long, hard look at the Givens and Goal.

In this problem, the Goal is clearly stated and does not provide any room for compromise or reformulation. Where the Givens are concerned, the obstacle could be removed if we took one of the experienced salespersons back to the old store with us, leaving the other one to carry on alone.

Many people fail to solve this problem because they *assume* that, once an experienced salesperson has been transferred to the new store, he or she must stay there. But the Givens set down no such limitations on their movement, so there is nothing to prevent you moving your sales-people back and forth between the two stores at will. The only conditions which have to be fulfilled are that there must never be more than five people at the old store and that unacceptable combinations of staff are avoided.

The solution tree makes obvious what might otherwise have been easily overlooked. A new initiative is required if any progress towards the Goal is to be made. Once this crucial insight has been attained, you can quickly and easily add two additional nodes to the tree (Figure 7.14, overleaf).

Only the left side of the tree has been developed so far, and I will deal with what would happen if the right node was expanded in a moment.

Do the new nodes meet *all* the conditions laid down in the problem? A quick check shows that no unacceptable combination of staff has occurred and that at no time are there more than five people in the old store.

The next step is to see what happens when you return to the new store, taking with you one of the experienced salespersons. This means that the two nodes can be expanded further to produce a total of four more. At

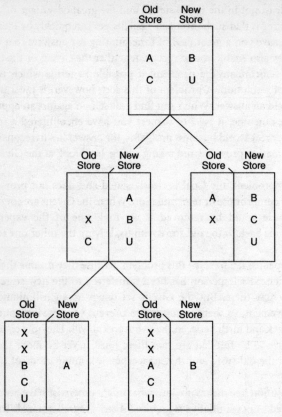

Figure 7.14 '... the next stage'

this point the tree can be pruned and simplified. The first thing to notice is that nodes (ii) and (iii) are identical, which means that only one of them needs to be considered further. But as they are also equivalent to the nodes two levels further back (arrowed), developing either of them further would be to return us to an earlier stage in the tree's growth.

A useful general rule when growing solution trees is to eliminate any nodes that duplicate earlier ones. The direction of movement should always be forward, towards the desired Goal, progress towards a solution, never regress back to the problem. Bearing this rule in mind, we can also discount node (iv), which is equivalent to an earlier node (arrowed).

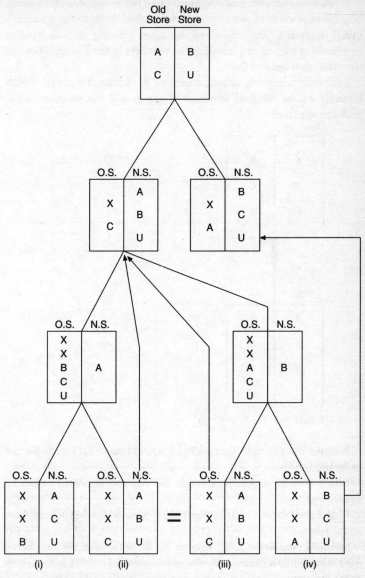

Figure 7.15 '. . . the next stage'

If you broke the rule and developed these two nodes, it would quickly become impossible to satisfy the conditions laid down in the problem's initial statement; you would end up either creating an unacceptable combination of staff or increasing the numbers in the old store beyond the maximum limit of five.

Your only remaining option, therefore, is to expand node (i), which instantly makes the final sequence of moves and the solution to the problem apparent.

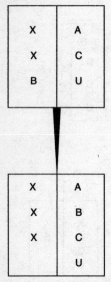

Figure 7.16 '*. . . thicker lines*'

Here the route from initial condition to final answer has been indicated using thicker lines.

Here's how the Operations which this tree has identified would be written out:

First-Level Node: You take Bill to the new store, leaving behind Alice and Charles.

Second-Level Node: After helping Bill to settle in at the new store, Alice is brought over and a new salesperson recruited to work with Charles at the old store.

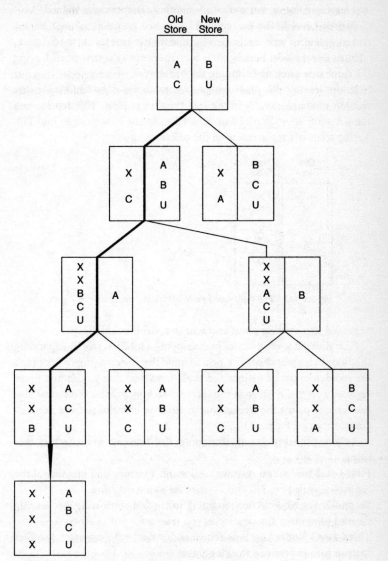

Figure 7.17 '... the next stage'

Third-Level Node: You return to the old store, taking Bill with you and leaving Alice on her own while another salesperson is trained.

Fourth-Level Node: You go back to the new premises, taking Charles, and complete his training, leaving Bill and the two new staff at the old store.

Fifth-Level Node: Finally Bill is brought over to the new store, leaving the three new sales staff running the old store.

Before leaving this problem, let's return to the right-hand node that was left incomplete early in the tree-creation process. This represented the situation after Charles had been taken to the new store to join Bill, having trained a replacement in the old store.

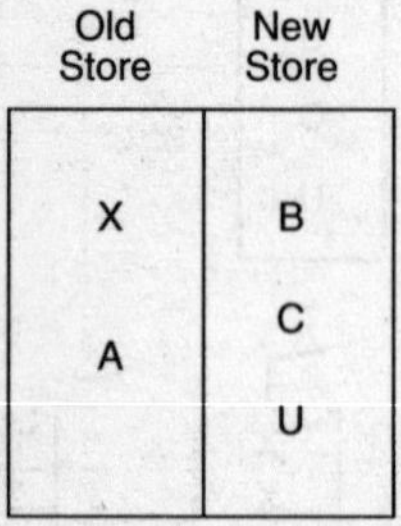

Old Store	New Store
X	B
	C
A	U

Figure 7.18 *'The right-hand node left incomplete earlier in Figure 7.14'*

Would this starting point also lead to a viable solution?

Give yourself some practice in developing a solution tree by expanding this node to see what happens. Bear in mind that forward progress through the problem must be maintained at all times, and that you should never regress to an earlier stage in the solution-seeking process. You must also take care to prune the tree as you go along in order to prevent needless complexity (see Figure 7.19).

As you probably found, this route also leads to a satisfactory solution.

First-Level Node: You start with Alice and a trainee staff member at the old store, while you, Bill and Charles are at the new one.

Second-Level Node: After returning to the old store with Bill, leaving Charles to manage the new store, you train a second salesperson.

Third-Level Node: You now return with Alice to the new store, so that she can gain experience working there.

Fourth-Level Node: Finally you travel to the old store for the last time to train another new staff member, before returning to the new store

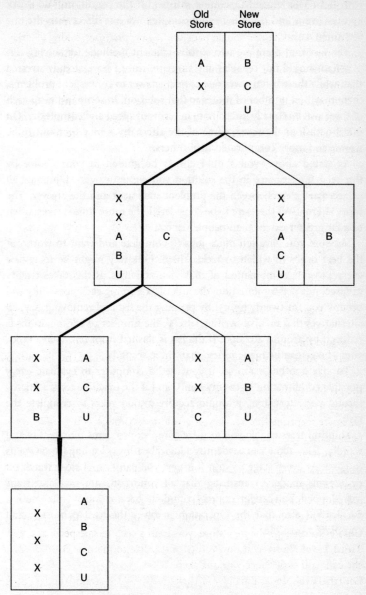

Figure 7.19 '*You must also take care to prune the tree . . .*'

with Bob. This second Operation satisfies all the conditions laid down by the Givens and is neither more complex nor less direct than the one identified earlier.

The fact that there are two equally efficient methods for solving this problem should not come as any surprise, since I have already stressed that, while there is only ever one correct answer to convergent problems, there may be a number of routes to that solution. In some instances each of these will be equally satisfactory in terms of speed and complexity. On other occasions, however, some of the alternatives may turn out to be slower and more complicated than others.

As stated above, you should always be guided in your choice by the need for elegance in the solution you come up with. Eliminate all unnecessary steps between the problem statement and the answer. The more alternatives there are to be considered, the more time it takes, often to a far greater extent than people realize.

Suppose you have ten office jobs to complete and want to work out the best order in which to tackle them. One way might be to review every possible combination of those ten activities. If this takes twenty milliseconds per combination, the task of examining each possibility will occupy you for twenty hours! By pruning the list and removing, say, all alternatives that involve 'writing letters', the number of combinations is reduced by around 400,000. If the list is slashed from ten to five tasks, your choice can be made in less than three seconds.

To give another example, if you used a computer to evaluate every possible combination of twenty items, and if the machine took a micro-second per alternative, it would require 77,000 years to complete the task.

Solution trees enable you to solve complex problems more easily and rapidly. They allow you to identify a logical pathway leading from Givens to Goal. At every stage of your journey, you can keep a close watch on deductions made, so ensuring that all conditions are met and traps side-stepped. You can feel entirely confident that not only is your solution correct but also that the Operation involves the least confusion and complexity possible.

SOLVING DIVERGENT PROBLEMS

As I have explained, this is a class of problem for which there is never a single correct solution. The key to success here is usually to break away from obvious answers and seek more creative ways of looking at all three elements, the Givens, Operations and Goals.

Divergent problems can also be approached by means of solution trees, a fact first demonstrated by Dr Karl Duncker, a pioneer in this field, whose studies of *functional fixedness* I have already described.

Forty years ago, when Duncker first started to explore divergent problems, an important clinical challenge was confronting cancer specialists. It was known that radiation was effective in killing inoperable stomach tumours. The problem was that this also killed the healthy surrounding tissue. The task, then, was to devise a method for destroying the cancerous tissue while leaving the healthy cells unharmed. This is clearly a divergent problem, since there are likely to be a number of possible solutions, some of which will be better, more practical or less hazardous than others. To construct this type of solution tree, you start by defining the problem in detail:

Problem Stage:

> How to destroy a tumour by means of radiation without harming surrounding healthy tissue.

Step two is to develop some general ideas about how such a problem might be tackled. You need not worry, for the moment, whether or not the answers you come up with are practical; this is something we will deal with further down in the solution tree. All you have to do at this early stage is to come up with proposals for what is termed the 'general range'. This includes all the answers that might just be possible, even though some may initially seem far-fetched and unworkable.

Where this problem is concerned, the two ideas most frequently made for the general range are shown in the second stage of the tree below.

Problem Stage:

> How to destroy a tumour by means of radiation without harming surrounding healthy tissue.

Stage Two: General Range

> Avoid contact between the rays and healthy tissue
> Reduce the strength of the rays as they pass through healthy tissue

At the third stage we seek out 'functional solutions', that is, methods by which ideas from the general range might be made to work. When these solutions are added to the tree, it assumes the shape shown in Figure 7.20.

I must make it clear that these are far from being the *only* possible ideas at the general range, nor does the diagram explore every possible functional solution. I have deliberately kept these to a minimum for the sake of creating an easy-to-follow illustration.

The fourth and final stage of tree building has now been reached. At this stage you have to discover specific methods by which the functional solutions could be put into practice. Your emphasis now is on devising practical techniques that will enable your earlier ideas to be implemented (see Figure 7.21, p. 146).

The five techniques listed there are those most frequently suggested, although, as before, they far from exhaust all the possibilities. When you come to consider the specific solutions in greater detail, you may well find that some are inappropriate while others would work with only a limited number of patients.

Of the solutions which Dr Duncker's problem-solving team came up with, the one that proved most useful was rotating the radiation source so that, while healthy tissues absorbed only a very low level, the tumour located at the centre received a constant bombardment.

When coming up with ideas at all stages of the tree's development, do not impose any kind of barrier on your thinking. Be as creative as you like and allow your creative juices free rein.

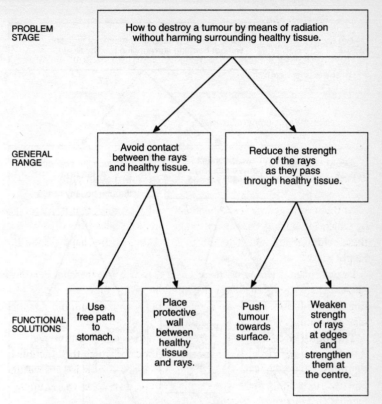

Figure 7.20 *'Solutions to tumour problems'*

DEVELOPING CREATIVE SOLUTIONS

Brainstorming is a widely used technique and a very effective method for coming up with creative ideas at all stages in the solution tree. There are four ground rules that must always be followed:

1. Criticism is ruled out.
2. Freewheeling is welcomed, the wilder the better – ideas are always easier to tame down than dream up.
3. Quantity, not quality, is wanted in the early stages. The more ideas

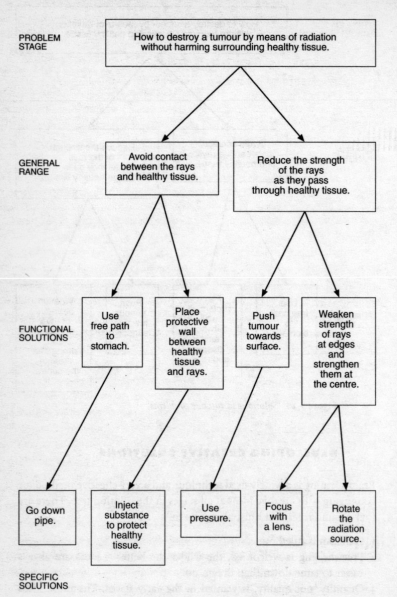

Figure 7.21 *'Practical techniques to solve problem'*

you can come up with, the higher the proportion of them that will be good ones.

4. Combination and improvement. Suggest how the ideas of others can be turned into better ideas.

Brainstorming with others is ideal, but you can also carry out your own one-person brainstorm. Relax as much as you can and consider the stage of the solution tree you have reached. Ask yourself: can I take what exists and:

adapt it – What else is like this; what other ideas does this suggest; what could I copy?

modify it – Add a new twist: change the meaning, colour, motion, sound, odour, form or shape?

magnify it – What could I add: more time, greater frequency, stronger, higher, longer, thicker, duplicate, exaggerate?

minimize it – What could I subtract, make smaller, condense, lower, shorten, lighten, omit, streamline, split up, understate?

substitute it – What else could I use instead; who else could I use instead; what other material, other processes, power, place, or approach could I use instead?

rearrange it – Can I interchange any components, change the pattern, lay-out, sequence, pace, schedule?

reverse it – Can I transpose positive and negative values, use opposites, turn it backwards, upside down, reverse roles, turn tables?

Finally, always see yourself as an efficient and successful problem-solver. This is not just a matter of boosting confidence and encouraging positive thinking, however valuable that may be. An intriguing study by Dr Ellen Langer of Harvard[4] suggests that even something as basic as having good eyesight is determined by who we believe ourselves to be! Her subjects were invited to become air force pilots for an afternoon. They were dressed in a pilot's uniform and given the chance to pilot a jet aircraft on a flight simulator. Everything was done to help them not just to play act as fliers but also to feel themselves to be genuine pilots. Before the experiment started, each participant was given a short physical examination, which included a routine eye test. During the flight simulation, while they were being pilots, they were asked to read the markings on the wings of another plane seen through the cockpit window. These markings were actually letters from an eye chart equivalent to the one used in the earlier physical. It was found that the vision of nearly half the pilots had improved significantly. Other groups of subjects, who were equally aroused and motivated but who were not immersed in the role, showed no such improvement. By changing the sense of self, it seems, we are able to understand the information around us in a more precise and intelligent manner.

SUMMARY

- Two important techniques for solving complicated convergent problems are creative carving and solution trees.
- In the first, you chop up big, complicated problems into smaller, simpler sub-problems that are easier to solve.
- When growing a solution tree, you reassemble the sub-problems in order to discover which Operations need to be performed in order to solve the main problem.
- The Operations you eventually identify should always be as simple as possible. The more complex they are, the easier it is to make a mistake when implementing them. Scientists speak of 'elegant' solutions, and this should also be the goal of those working in business and commerce.
- Divergent problems can often be solved more easily through brainstorming. During such sessions, the ideas you start out with can be as improbable and apparently far-fetched as you like. The more ideas you generate, the more good ideas you will come up with.
- Try turning problems around and looking at them from different angles. Think about all the ways the Given might be changed in order to achieve the desired goal.

8

How to Make Better Decisions

> 'Nothing is so exhausting as indecision, and nothing is so futile.'
>
> Bertrand Russell, *The Conquest of Happiness* (1930)

The French philosopher Jean-Paul Sartre's comment that: 'I am my choices' emphasizes the crucial role of decision-making in shaping our lives.

When reaching judgements, most people like to imagine that they are basing their decisions on a logical evaluation of all the main issues, both for and against each available option, and that they are not being unduly swayed by emotions, prejudices and faulty conclusions. When any of these decisions turns out to be mistaken or misguided, blame is often laid on external influences beyond our control, on bad timing, bad advice or plain bad luck. What we seldom appreciate is that our decision-making is fraught with numerous – but avoidable – snags and traps. It is these, more often than not, that lead us into faulty choices.

The more information we must deal with when reaching a decision, and the less time we have to reflect on the issues, the more likely that we shall act unwisely.

Research has indicated that there are three main styles of decision-making. When able to use our preferred style, we make decisions more easily and with less anxiety than if obliged to adopt one of the other two styles.

Before describing what these styles are, check your own approach to decision-making by completing the questionnaire below.

DISCOVER YOUR DECISION-MAKING STYLE

Assess this by deciding how you would respond in each of the four situations described:

Situation No. 1

A stockbroker friend gives you hot tips on three high-risk, high-yield shares. You take a chance and invest in the first. Within days you sell again at an excellent profit. Delighted by this success, you use your windfall to purchase the second tipped share. Once again you make a killing. What will you do about tip number three?

A. Put all your profits on the third share. If it proves as accurate as his other two, you will be very rich indeed.
B. Rest content with your present gains and not risk even a portion of the profits.
C. Invest only part of your earnings. You will still see an excellent return on the initial investment, without any risk of losing everything, if tip number three proves inaccurate.

Situation No. 2

You are about to leave home at the start of a day which will take you out and about. Because much of your travel will be done on foot, it's important to take note of the weather. Although the sky is clear at present, the forecast warned of heavy rain to come. You will have to take a briefcase and a lap-top computer with you, so carrying an umbrella is going to prove awkward. Also, because the day is humid, wearing a raincoat will be uncomfortable. Which of the following thoughts is likely to be running through your mind as you prepare for work?

A. The forecast is often wrong and the sky looks bright and clear. I'll take a chance on fine weather and leave both the umbrella and raincoat at home.
B. It always seems to rain when I'm unwise enough to leave my

umbrella and raincoat at home. Despite the fact that they'll add to my discomfort if it stays fine, I'd better take both along.

C. I would feel a fool if the heavens opened and I got drenched. On the other hand, taking along both an umbrella and a raincoat does seem unnecessary. I'll compromise by leaving the coat at home and taking just the umbrella with me. That way, if it stays fine I would not be too encumbered, while if it rains I'll enjoy at least some protection from the elements.

Situation No. 3

You've just landed an excellent job in another part of the country and are having to move home. Because you are paying a high interest rate on a bridging loan to buy the new house, it is important that you dispose of your old one rapidly. The property business is going through one of its periodic downturns and houses in your neighbourhood are selling slowly. The agent advises that your asking price of £85,000 is fair and realistic.

Two days after your house goes on the market, a prospective purchaser arrives, falls in love with your property and offers £78,000. He insists that this is his final offer, and he will not negotiate. Although way below your asking price, the good news is that he has no house of his own to sell and can pay you in cash immediately.

By accepting his offer, you will lose money on the transaction, since your new home is costing you £82,000. On the other hand, if your house fails to sell for some time, interest rates will mean that you could lose even more. Are you most likely to:

A. reject the deal because it involves too great a loss?
B. accept the offer for fear that your house will not find another ready buyer and you will be worse off due to interest charges?
C. try to keep the buyer interested while stalling him for a few weeks in the hope of a better offer from another purchaser?

Situation No. 4

Your company's success has always depended on the drive and motivation of a young and ambitious sales force. You learn that the sales director of a competitor company has just resigned. You also know that his experience and marketing knowledge could prove a tremendous asset to your own organization. Your problem is that it is unclear exactly why he resigned. A statement from the other company attributes it to policy differences following a recent merger. His version is that he and his new MD had a clash of personalities. The grapevine suggests that either the man has a serious drink problem or he had been caught out defrauding his last company; rumours claim that they agreed not to prosecute provided he resigned at once. It is possible, however, that this is deliberate misinformation spread by his last firm in the hope of discouraging rivals from employing him.

After a lengthy interview, you are still not certain of the truth. He sticks to his story and angrily refutes suggestions of either alcoholism or fraud.

If the background is merely a case of malicious gossip, he will prove a tremendous asset to your company by significantly increasing sales. If it is true, he could demoralize and demotivate your sales force to such an extent that profits could be slashed and future prosperity jeopardized. On the other hand, if you do not employ him and a rival company does, this too could adversely affect your future prospects. Which of the following courses are you most likely to adopt?

A. Give him the job. He will be such a tremendous asset to your company that it's worth taking a risk and ignoring unsubstantiated rumours.
B. Decline to employ him. The risk is too great and it is better to be safe than sorry when taking such an important decision.
C. Play for time by explaining that you are very interested in employing him but cannot make an immediate offer. In the breathing space, take whatever steps are necessary to check out the allegations to determine for sure whether or not there is any truth in them.

Now total up the number of A, B, and C statements ticked. If you ticked mostly 'A' responses, you have a gambler's style of decision-making. If you ticked mainly 'B' responses, you have a fireman's style of decision-making. If you ticked mainly 'C' responses, you have a tight-rope walker's style of decision-making.

Choosing a mixed bag of responses indicates a flexible approach that allows you to modify your approach, depending on the type of decision being taken.

YOUR DECISION-MAKING STYLE IN ACTION

GAMBLER

In any risky situation you prefer the option which promises the greatest gains, should things go your way. This style is typical of an entrepreneur who is always ready to take a chance if the reward looks sufficiently tempting. Gamblers are highly optimistic about their ability to come out on top, no matter how adverse their circumstances may seem. When they make a wrong decision, little time is wasted on regrets or recriminations. Instead, such setbacks are looked on as a valuable learning experience.

If you place yourself in this category of decision-maker, you will be at your best when faced with a situation in which all the options appear equally unattractive. This is because you will be acutely sensitive to anything positive in any of the courses of action. The likelihood of good things occurring as a result of making a particular decision will be immediately apparent to you, while you will feel less intimidated by the negative outcomes. The obvious weakness of such a 'winner takes all' strategy is that big gains are frequently matched by equally large losses.

When faced with too much information on which to make your decisions, you have a tendency to act impulsively and impatiently, eschewing logical, objective analysis for gut reactions and intuitions. The more information you have at your disposal, the less likely you are to take the time and trouble to analyse it carefully. You are at greatest risk of falling foul of the trap of Gambler's Fallacy (see below). Research suggests that around one in five managers adopt a gambler style of decision-making.

FIREMAN

The essential feature of this decision-making style is the powerful desire to reduce the risk of loss to a minimum. Like the famous Captain Murphy, who originated Murphy's Law, these decision-makers are of the opinion that 'if something can go wrong it will go wrong'. Their approach is always to choose the option most likely to safeguard them when the worst happens. This style of decision-making is ideally suited to very high-risk decisions where there is a strong possibility of material or financial loss, for instance when dealing on the stock or currency markets.

When the odds against a successful outcome are high, a fireman's decision-making style is not only safest but stands the best chance of ensuring a steady if unspectacular gain. The weakness of this approach is that valuable opportunities may be overlooked and that, in attempts to minimize losses, the full potential of a situation may never be exploited.

The main threat from information overload lies in a reluctance to commit oneself to any course of action before all the risks have been fully identified and analysed. Since this state of perfect knowledge can never be achieved, the fireman is especially vulnerable to the 'paralysis of analysis', a state of procrastination in which nothing ever seems to get done (see below). Studies suggest that one-third of managers adopt this style of decision-making.

TIGHT-ROPE WALKER

The main desire of those who possess this style is to protect themselves, and others, from decisions that will cause later regrets. They look for the option that will allow them to salvage as much as possible from the situation, should things go wrong, and to make the most of any gains if the decision proves a wise one. Technically, they seek to minimize their maximum loss and maximize their minimum gain.

Of the three styles, the tight-rope walker is most sensitive to discrepancies between what has been achieved and what might have been achieved had a different decision been taken. If this is your preferred decision-making style, you will regard lost opportunities and missed chances as such a cause for regret and frustration that you will try to find ways of keeping them to a minimum. Your best decisions are made in situations where there is great uncertainty. Where outcomes are clouded in doubt, your middle-of-the-road approach can provide the safest and most successful course of action. If the decision turns out badly, losses are kept to a minimum; if it turns out well, you will still make positive gains.

Because information overload typically provides so much evidence both for and against any particular option, it can cause much concern and stress among managers and professionals who favour this decision-making style. Research suggests that four out of ten managers employ this style.

Most people intuitively know which of these three styles they feel most comfortable with and which they are likely to adopt under any given circumstances. Some of you may vary your decision-making style from one situation to the next, and this is all to the good.

As I have explained, each approach has its strengths and weaknesses, and these should be appreciated in order to remove a potential source of bias from your decision-making. By understanding what causes you to respond in a particular way, you can ensure that your approach will match the demands of a specific decision. It also allows you to identify the approach used by others involved in the decision-making and, when this would be to your advantage, to exploit the weakness or appreciate the strength of their chosen style.

DECISION-MAKING AND TIME PRESSURES

One of the most obvious effects of information overload is that it reduces the amount of time available for use when making decisions. Busy managers and professionals often come under tremendous pressure to reach a decision, even a complex and important one, in a very short space of time. This time pressure has a crucial and damaging influence on our abilities to think through all the available options and to reach a balanced viewpoint.

In order to understand why this happens, I'd like you to imagine yourself trapped in a waking nightmare. It is two a.m. and you have just woken up in your hotel bedroom on the twenty-fourth floor of a Manhattan skyscraper. Moments before, you had been having a terrifying dream: you were trapped by a raging inferno, hundreds of metres above the ground. As you fumble sleepily for the light switch, you realize that the dream is all too terribly true. You smell and see the wisps of dark smoke seeping under the bedroom door. From the bedrooms on either side you can hear horrified cries. Placing a hand against your bedroom door, you feel heat penetrating the woodwork, indicating that the corridor is ablaze. Looking through the picture windows, you see flames leaping from the floors above. The panoramic view of the New York skyline, which had appeared so inspiring when you checked in earlier that evening, now merely emphasizes your isolation and danger.

Your survival could well depend on the decisions you make in the next few minutes. What will you decide to do?

1. Stay in your room?
2. Make a frantic dash for freedom along the blazing corridor?
3. Attempt to lower yourself, using knotted sheets, to another bedroom that is still free from flames?
4. Curl up in a foetal position in the bathroom and hope for the best?
5. Seal the spaces around the door with wet towels and wait to be rescued?
6. Leap to certain death rather than face the agony of being burned alive?

All the above are decisions made by people in similar predicaments. Which one you are most likely to opt for depends on a number of variables, including your age, aspects of your personality and how calm you can remain in a crisis. But whenever we are obliged to make decisions under stress, research suggests that the choices we make also depend crucially on how much time we have to decide.

Studies by Irving Janis, Professor of Psychology at Yale University, suggest that decision-making often follows the pattern of thinking illustrated below in Figure 8.1. Although this diagram may appear somewhat complex, its logic is easy to follow, and the insights it provides, especially where information overload is concerned, make the effort well worth while.

To understand how the process works, imagine yourself on a garage forecourt looking at some second-hand cars. A salesman approaches and asks if you are interested in changing your car. This is what Janis describes in his chart as an 'opportunity'. At its most dramatic, his second entry into the decision process, 'challenging negative feedback', would be finding yourself trapped by the hotel fire!

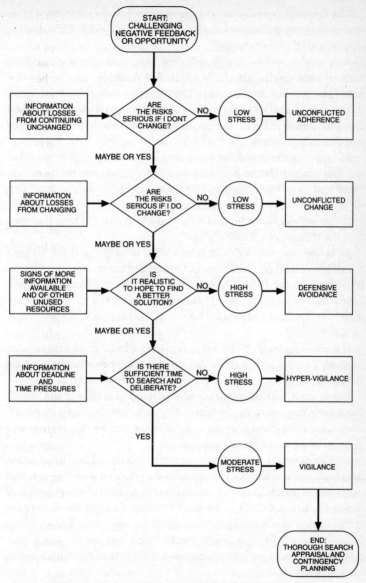

Figure 8.1 *'Flowchart: opportunity-challenging negative feedback' The conflict-theory model of decision making* (after Janis & Mann, 1977: 70)[1]

The first step is to decide whether you need to decide at all. This is shown in the first diamond-shaped decision box, which asks: 'Are the risks serious if I don't change?'

As a prudent motorist, you will need to find out the likely costs of keeping your current vehicle. If a qualified mechanic assures you that your present vehicle is in excellent condition and unlikely to break down in the near future, you may well decide not to spend money on a new car. Such a decision is called 'unconflicted adherence'. It is easily made and creates little stress.

But suppose the reason for wandering around the garage forecourt in the first place is because a mechanic has warned you that your car could well soon break down and would then require costly repairs? This statement, about the loss of not changing, takes us down the flowchart to the second decision diamond box, where your next question becomes: 'Are the risks serious if I do change?'

As before, you will seek out information to help you make up your mind. How much do I know about the make of car on offer? How many miles has it done? Does it have a full service history? Does that model have a reputation for reliability? How much do I know about the garage itself? Do they have a reputation for selling roadworthy, value-for-money vehicles?

If it all looks good, if the car is fairly priced and comes through an engineer's report with a clean sheet, you will probably decide to make the change with little stress, a response called 'unconflicted change'.

But suppose you find yourself in what psychologists call a 'double-bind'. Put simply, this means you're damned if you do and damned if you don't. Your current vehicle is in a poor state of repair, but the only replacement you can afford looks equally unreliable.

Moving down the chart to the third decision diamond box, the question now becomes 'Is it realistic to hope to find a better solution?' So you seek out information about other possible options. Could I borrow the money to buy a better car? Can I find a more reliable vehicle for the same price? Is my own car capable of being repaired? If the answer to these questions is 'No', you will be in a highly stressful state and one in which your powers of reasoning will be undermined. This state of mind is known as 'defensive avoidance'.

Returning to our hotel fire, Professor Janis's analysis suggests we might first ask ourselves 'Can I remain where I am?' If the answer appears to be 'No', because you risk being burned alive or suffocated by smoke, your next question will be: 'Can I escape?' If the answer again appears to be 'No', you will desperately seek out a third course of action. If you are unable to think of one, you might resort to 'defensive avoidance' by closing your eyes and hoping to wake up, to find it really was just a nightmare! Rescue workers know all too well that the first response of many disaster victims is to 'freeze' and make no attempt to save themselves. I shall say more about defensive avoidance in relation to information overload in a moment.

But it is with the fourth decision diamond box, 'Is there sufficient time to search and deliberate?', that the real crunch comes! If you know that your hotel door, constructed to modern specifications, is capable of holding back the flames for several hours, the answer to this question could well be 'Yes'. Knowing you have a good chance of being rescued should arouse only moderate levels of stress and produce a state of vigilance in which you can think clearly and act decisively.

You stack wet towels around the door frame to keep out the smoke, you attract attention to your plight by using the telephone or hanging towels out of the window, you wrap a wet towel around your mouth and nose, keep low and wait for rescue. Such calm and considered decisions could well save your life.

If, however, you are convinced that your bedroom is about to be engulfed in flames, you are far more likely to be so highly stressed that you experience hyper-vigilance. In this confused and panic-stricken state you may make fatal and irrational decisions, such as leaping from the window to certain death.

As Irving Janis explains: 'Warnings that arouse intense emotional reactions can lead to resistance to change, misattributions, erroneous judgements, and defective decisions, sometimes as a result of panic or extreme reactions of defensive avoidance.'[2]

Making a decision under the pressures of information overload is seldom this dramatic, but it can just as easily give rise to faulty decision-making as a result of defensive avoidance and hyper-vigilance.

Defensive Avoidance

This can involve:

- procrastination
- shifting responsibility for the decision-making to others
- denying that any decision needs to be made
- dismissing reasons for change as irrelevant or unimportant.

An example of defensive avoidance is the refusal of many organizations to face up to the threat of the so-called Millennium Bug. Actually this is not a bug at all but has arisen because programmers have routinely used only the final two digits to represent a year in dates, hence 29 meant 1929. This works fine up to the end of the year 1999, at which point all hell is predicted to break loose as computers interpret 'oo' not as 2000 but as 1900. This is sometimes called the Year 2000 or Y2K problem, a crisis which *Byte* magazine has described as: 'A crisis without precedent in human history. We know when it's going to occur. We also know that its effects will be global. We even know what's causing it and what to do about it . . . We can, if we all choose, solve it before it happens, although we probably won't.'[3] If something isn't done about the problem, the result is likely to be chaos, with computers – from those running banks and pharmaceutical companies to those involved in air traffic control – producing random and unpredictable errors.

The whole world has been aware of this major glitch in computer hardware, software and data for several years, yet a majority of organizations have failed to respond with sufficient urgency, and many did not respond at all. 'All told,' warns the influential magazine, *Business Week*, 'the Year 2000 bug could cost the US about $119 billion in lost economic output between now and 2001.'[4]

Defensive avoidance can be seen as having played a role in the faulty decision-making which led to such inertia. Some managers procrastinated or tried shifting responsibility to manufacturers and suppliers; others denied that there was any problem, while a significant proportion even dismissed it all as a hoax, mere hype put about by consultants and software vendors in order to make money. If your company depends on computers and has adopted any of the above strategies, then take to the lifeboats. Your vessel is about to strike an iceberg!

Paradoxically, the vast amounts of information now potentially available through computer systems have made the likelihood of resorting to defensive avoidance more rather than less likely. This is for three reasons:

- With so many facts and figures to choose from, some decision-makers experience the 'paralysis of analysis'. They become so concerned about having missed a vital piece of information that they retreat into inactivity as a protection against the possibility of making a mistake.
- Those who take refuge in denial can usually find evidence in support of their standpoint if they search long and hard enough.
- Procrastination can be disguised as diligence and an insistence that even more time must be spent searching for additional information.

Research suggests that over two-thirds of managers collect very large quantities of information when making decisions, even though four out of ten of them also admit to wasting a great deal of time locating such information. As one of them put it: 'I doubt whether the value of information received is worth the time spent accumulating it.'

All of these justifications for delay and indecision should be exposed for what they so often are: examples of defensive avoidance rather than logical reasons for not deciding.

Vigilance and Hyper-vigilance

When we are in a vigilant state of mind, we are best able to search diligently for relevant information, which is then assessed in an unbiased manner, with each option carefully appraised, before a decision is made. As a result, our judgements are most likely to be sound and rational.

By contrast, in a panicky state of hyper-vigilance, a decision-maker 'searches frantically for a way out of the dilemma, rapidly shifts back and forth between alternatives, and impulsively seizes upon a hastily contrived solution that seems to promise immediate relief. He or she overlooks the full range of consequences of his or her choice because of emotional excitement, repetitive thinking and cognitive constriction.'[5] (By this last phrase, Professor Janis means highly simplified, limited and unproductive reasoning.) An example of the catastrophic decisions that can be made under extreme stress occurred in January 1989 when a British Midland 737 crashed just short of the East Midlands Airport in England, killing forty-four of the 126 passengers aboard. This happened when the left engine failed and, while attempting an emergency landing at the airport, the pilot mistakenly shut down the right engine, which until then was still functioning.

Information overload increases the risk of hyper-vigilance in two key ways:

● by making so much information potentially available that there is often a lurking doubt that one has missed some crucial fact or figure when making a decision. In the words of one manager: 'It's reached the stage where you cannot come to a decision without worrying that someone might have more information than you and could make your decision look wrong.'
● by imposing time pressures and deadlines on the search for the best options.

SIX TRAPS YOU MUST AVOID

Although we like to think of ourselves as highly rational and logical individuals, who base our decisions on a diligent analysis of all the relevant options, the worrying truth is that as a general rule we do not. Even judgements made in a calm and relaxed state of mind are frequently irrational and based on a misunderstanding of the available information.

While all decision-makers need to be aware of the potential biases and pitfalls in their decision-making, it becomes even more important for workers facing the dual pressures of relentless deadlines and information overload.

There are six main ways in which we can blunder when taking decisions.

1. MISINTERPRETATION

It is essential to have a clear understanding of the information guiding your decision, since this determines how you interpret it. Suppose you are on a jury hearing a case of alleged sexual assault. The only scientific evidence linking the accused, a US president, and his alleged victim, a former White House intern, is a sample of semen. Found on the victim's skirt, it matches a DNA sample from the accused. You hear evidence that the probability of the president's DNA producing a match by chance is 0.1 per cent. On this evidence alone, would you decide to convict or acquit?

Now imagine the same trial and the same evidence, only this time you are told that one in a thousand men in Washington, DC, could have produced such a match. Are you more or less likely to come to a verdict of guilty?

When Dr Jonathan Koehle, a psychologist at the University of Texas at Austin, conducted this exact experiment with two groups of mock jurors, he discovered that how the evidence was presented made a big difference to the decision reached. Although the two statements mean exactly the same thing, the effect on the jury was dramatic. When told the probability of a match by chance was 0.1 per cent, 28 per cent decided the president was guilty. Informed that one man in a thousand could have left the semen stain, only 8 per cent did so. Koehle believes that frequencies (1 in 1000) are easier to understand than percentages (0.1 per cent). 'I think people have a very hard time distinguishing between numbers like 0.1 per cent and 0.01 per cent,' he says.

This view is supported by the fact that, when asked how many people in a city of 500,000 would have DNA samples matching the president's, 74 per cent answered correctly. When given the number as a percentage (0.1 per cent) only 26 per cent got it right.[6]

If you too have to make important decisions based largely on numerical evidence, be very sure you fully understand the figures before deciding.

2. THE BASE-RATE EFFECT

This is another common cause of misinterpretation. Imagine that you are going out on a family picnic and rain has been forecast. Although you will be sitting in the open air for only around an hour, you know the accuracy of such reports is 80 per cent. Since the chances of your family getting soaked appear to be eight out of ten, you clutter yourselves up with raincoats and umbrellas. A sensible decision? Probably not, since the chances of it actually raining are not eight out of ten, but closer to one-third.

As mathematician Robert Matthews explains:[7] 'This strange result has nothing to do with forecasters making exaggerated claims, or with the innate cussedness of the climate. It's an example of a curious mathematical effect that can trip up any attempt to make sense of uncertain data, from forecasts of relatively trivial matters such as rainfall to predictions of earthquakes or testimony of witnesses in a murder trial.'

Known as 'the base-rate effect', it is the effect that the chances of an event happening at all has on our ability to make rational decisions based on our predictions of it happening. As Matthews makes clear: 'Even when you think you are making very accurate predictions, your correct forecasts of the rare event can be swamped by a huge number of failures.'

Returning to the picnic above, since forecasts by the British Meteorological Forecasts Office are around 80 per cent accurate, it seems reasonable to assume that, if they say it will rain, they are going to be right eight times out of ten.

But this ignores the base-rate of rain over a one-hour period, which, in Britain, is around 0.1. This means that during your hour-long picnic there will be just one chance in ten of getting a soaking. So your decision to take an umbrella and raincoat to be on the safe side will prove ill-advised nine times out of ten.

Suppose you and your family go on 100 hour-long picnics per year. The hourly base-rate for rain means that on ninety of these journeys no rain will fall (100 × 0.9), while on the remaining ten you would be wise to carry an umbrella.

With a forecast accuracy of 80 per cent, rain will be accurately predicted on eight of these ten occasions. But an 80 per cent accuracy, impressive though it may be, also means that it will stay dry on 20 per cent of the picnics for which rain is forecast. As a result, you will be warned of rain to come on 20 per cent of the ninety outings made, when in fact no rain falls. On these eighteen outings (20 per cent of 90) your decision to carry an umbrella will be wrong.

This makes a total of twenty-six occasions when rain is forecast, of which just eight turn out to be accurate. In other words, the base-rate effect means that the decisions you take are based on a prediction accuracy not of 80 per cent but of just 30 per cent.

Going out for such a short length of time means that, statistically, it is never necessary to carry an umbrella, even when torrential rain is forecast. If you intend to stay out in the open longer than one hour, however, the chances of getting caught in a forecast downpour increase significantly. In the UK the daily (as opposed to the hourly) base rate of rain is 0.4, giving you a four-in-ten chance of being drenched. The more frequently an event occurs, the easier it becomes to make accurate forecasts and sensible decisions.

The base-rate effect for hourly rain becomes easier to understand if one creates a table of the different values (in terms of percentages).

	Rain	No rain	Total
Rain predicted	8	18	26
No rain predicted	2	72	74
Total	10	90	100

A widely used demonstration of the base-rate effect is the so-called 'cab problem'. Imagine a town in which cabs come in only two colours: 15 per cent are blue and 85 per cent are green. One dark night, a cab is involved in a hit-and-run accident. An eye-witness claims that the cab was blue. Police conduct a series of experiments that show that the witness can accurately identify the colour of cabs at night on eight out of ten occasions. A jury is assembled and the driver of a blue cab is arrested and found guilty, purely on the evidence of the eye-witness. But how reliable is that evidence? The answer most usually given is around 80 per cent; after all, in the police tests, their witness was correct eight times out of ten.

The real answer, which can be simply demonstrated using a contingency table similar to the one above for the rain decision, shows his true accuracy to be less than half (41 per cent, to be exact). This is because the far higher number of green cabs in the town (85 per cent are green) means that the chances of the eye-witness being confused by the two colours overwhelm his success in identifying cabs which really are blue. With a less than 50/50 chance of their witness being accurate, the police would get a fairer result by tossing a coin.

What do studies like this tell us about decision-making under the pressures of information overload? Simply that you must never jump to conclusions, especially when rare events are involved, and that, in such cases, knowing how the base-rate effect can skew your thinking, asking the right questions becomes of critical importance.

3. GAMBLER'S FALLACY

Peter has been playing the roulette wheel for several hours without much luck. Over the past twelve spins, he's noticed that black has come up eleven times. 'That's a long run of blacks,' he reasons. 'The chances have to be high that a red will come up on the next spin.' So that's where he puts his money. A sensible decision? Not really. In fact Peter has just fallen victim to Gambler's Fallacy.

Although all roulette players lose in the long run, owing to the presence of zero on the wheel and the odds that casinos pay out, victims of this widespread fallacy hand over their money more rapidly than most. Why this is so, I'll explain in a moment. But for now, let's explore the strategy Peter is using in order to understand why it must fail.

The roulette wheel has no memory, no way of keeping tally of the number of times it has rewarded one colour against the other. As I and my co-author, James Greene, explained in an earlier book on efficient thinking: 'The odds of red coming up after a run of eleven black numbers, or eleven hundred or eleven thousand, or any number, is exactly the same as it was before the wheel ever began to spin.'[8] In theory, those odds would be 50:50; in practice, the odds are deliberately reduced by casino bosses to ensure that the house will always make a profit in the long run.

It is the same with tossing a coin. Provided there are no built-in biases in the coin or the way it is tossed, the fact that it has landed heads 100 times in succession makes no difference to the chances of its landing either heads or tails on the 101st toss. However much common sense might seem to support the view that 'it's bound to come up tails on the next toss', the chances remain exactly the same as on the first toss, 50:50. Believe otherwise and you have fallen foul of Gambler's Fallacy.

Although this particular hazard conjured up images of Las Vegas casinos, it can be found wherever rapid, high-risk decisions have to be taken under conditions of uncertainty. 'We've lost money on the last three investments,' the financial director admits, 'so it must be about time to get lucky with this new proposal!' Instead of analysing his earlier decisions and searching for logical reasons why the last three projects all failed, the director is trusting to luck and, by doing so, become yet another victim of the fatal Gambler's Fallacy.

Although a common cause of faulty decision-making, the Fallacy is even

more widespread among workers suffering from information overload –
and for one very good reason. All too often the amount of information
that has to be considered, when combined with deadline pressures to
make decisions in a hurry, allows insufficient time to identify all the
possible options and evaluate their likely consequences objectively. Under
these circumstances, the temptation to depend on luck, intuition and
hunches becomes ever more powerful. We turn to anything, in fact, that
will enable us to reach a decision, however ill-advised it later turns out
to be.

4. GUESSER'S DISADVANTAGE

You've been invited to take part in a simple gambling game with a friend.
One of you will toss a coin while the other bets on how it will land.
Should you choose to toss the coin or place the bet?

The answer is: you should always toss the coin, since, even when it is
a fair coin fairly tossed, making the decision under such conditions places
you at a disadvantage.

As I explained above, a fair coin fairly tossed has an equal chance of
landing either heads or tails. Anybody betting on the outcome in a purely
random fashion, therefore, could be expected to guess correctly half the
time. Indeed, were the number of correct guesses significantly higher or
lower than 50 per cent, one could suspect that the decision-making was
non-random; it would indicate the presence of a bias which, for some
reason, was causing the better to be more or less accurate in his or her
guesses than chance alone dictates.

To study this effect, scientists programmed a computer to present
either the word 'heads' or 'tails' on a monitor in a completely random
fashion. Using a computer instead of a real coin enabled them to eliminate
any bias. Volunteers, who sat in front of the computer screen, were asked
to anticipate what the next 'call' would be by pressing one of two buttons.
Since the words were flashed up randomly, subjects who were able to
guess in an equally random manner should have been right 50 per cent
of the time. But that was not what the scientists found. In practice, most
volunteers guess significantly below the rate of success that chance alone
would have dictated. Although they all knew that to obtain a 50 per cent
success-rate they had to press the buttons randomly, a pattern was always

present, and this distorted the results. However hard they tried to distribute their guesses evenly between heads and tails, one or the other was being consistently favoured.

You might argue that I explained why this happens in my discussion of Gambler's Fallacy. Given a run of heads, for instance, a player might be tempted to press the 'tails' button on the mistaken assumption that this was now a more likely outcome. While it is true that the Fallacy does involve a pattern of decision-making and probably plays a role in Guesser's Disadvantage, it is by no means the only factor involved. Even when the scientists controlled for the Fallacy, their subjects continued making guesses below chance level; in other words, a pattern of thinking was making their decisions non-random. No matter how hard they tried to distribute their guesses evenly between heads and tails, one or other was still consistently favoured.

To understand why such patterns occur, try the following experiment. For the next fifteen seconds, do your utmost not to think of the phrase 'information overload'. You will find it quite impossible.

We cannot, at any moment in our lives, whether waking or sleeping, switch off the train of thoughts racing through our mind. It is this powerful flow of ideas, this constant current of mental activity, that determines the course of our decision-making. However hard we strive to pluck options from thin air at random, and no matter how sincerely we believe this to be true, such hopes are a mere illusion. Guesswork is not what it seems, a purely random selection from alternative options; rather, it is the result of patterns of mental responses, many of which operate below the level of awareness. As Thomas Brown put it when trying to explain his decision to dislike his headmaster, Dr John Fell:

> I do not like thee, Doctor Fell,
> The reason why I cannot tell;'
> But this I know, and know full well,
> I do not like thee, Doctor Fell.[9]

As with many aspects of gambling, Guesser's Disadvantage offers us some practical insights into the nature of mistakes made in business decisions. It can lead, for example, to a series of options being chosen in the face of all logic, common sense and experience. This is particularly likely to occur when the brain is already befuddled by information overload.

Become aware of this hazard whenever you are faced with a risky decision in conditions of great uncertainty. Understand that forces are operating within your brain of which you may remain blissfully unaware. Seek out the underlying pattern in your choices, then work to develop more effective and productive strategies in the future. Never be tempted to attribute a series of fortunate decisions to the 'fact' that you are passing through a lucky phase. The most reliable and rewarding approach is to identify the ways in which these choices were made and then to adopt them when making future decisions.

5. THE RISKY SHIFT

A camel, so the joke goes, is a 'horse designed by a committee'. This reflects the widespread belief that, while individuals acting alone are enterprising and audacious risk-takers, caution replaces initiative and risk-taking vanishes the moment they come together in a group. In fact, the opposite is true. Groups of people are actually more likely to take risky decisions than people working alone. Known as the 'Risky Shift', this move away from caution, which occurs whenever people make collective decisions, was first identified by Dr James Stoner at the Massachusetts Institute of Technology[10] during the late 1960s.

In his studies, people were first asked to make individual decisions as to what should be done about imaginary characters in various stories. A number of options were suggested with varying degrees of risk and reward; in each case, a higher risk was linked to a greater reward. After deciding what course of action the fictitious characters should adopt, the subjects were brought together to take a group decision for the same set of characters in identical circumstances. When making their choices independently, most subjects selected middle-of-the-road options which combined moderate levels of risk with modest rewards. But when deciding as a group, the majority of subjects shifted ground significantly, and now favoured high-risk/high-reward choices. Stoner found that collective choice always involved the greater gamble, with decisions ranging from the slightly rash to the completely foolhardy.

Why the Risky Shift occurs is not known for certain, although diffusion of responsibility (wherein no single individual can be blamed if the decision turns out to be wrong) and peer-group pressures probably play a part. In groups of male decision-makers especially, there may be a desire to 'out-macho' the next guy by raising the stakes and supporting increasingly gung-ho choices.

When large groups of people are brought together electronically, as happens if decisions are made through Intranet collaborations, the danger of the Risky Shift leading to incredibly imprudent decisions increases significantly. A tragic example of this can be seen in the Challenger disaster in 1986, when the space shuttle exploded as a result, it was later discovered, of rubber seals becoming brittle after a night of below-zero temperatures. As the late Richard Feynman, the physicist who identified the problem, clearly demonstrated, concerns by individual engineers at the company manufacturing these vital 'O'-ring seals were overruled by group decisions to proceed. While a range of factors contributed to the final, fatal launch decision, it seems likely that the Risky Shift also played a leading role.

Protect your decisions against this very real hazard by:

● warning group members about the Risky Shift
● asking each participant to arrive at an individual decision before taking part in group decision-making. Then try to ensure that none of them is swayed too far from his or her original choice.
● Prepare your own decision, prior to any meeting, by using one of the two procedures described below.

The best decisions are those reached through consensus. Studies have shown them to be more effective than those reached by the majority, the minority or a single individual.

6. THE PARALYSIS OF ANALYSIS

The value of any information is directly proportional to the expense of making a poor decision or the reward associated with making a good one.

When gathering evidence in support of a decision, there comes a point when each extra hour spent searching for additional facts has a cost in wasted time that outweighs any benefits gained. The search for evidence can also turn into a displacement activity whose purpose (whether or not this is consciously recognized at the time) is to divert you away from the more stressful task of deciding. Information overload reinforces this tendency to avoid difficult challenges, since there is always going to be more information 'out there' on the Internet than you have managed to collect. The result can be so-called 'paralysis of analysis', a desire to keep seeking out information long after this need has passed.

When deciding how far to go and how deeply to dig in the quest for knowledge, you need to decide on the likely consequences of a 'best' and a 'worst' case. If the most extreme consequences of a decision would have only a trivial impact on the outcome of events, whether for good or for ill, then little effort need be expended in gathering information before a decision is made. If, however, the worst or best outcome would have a major impact on the future, then it is reasonable to spend considerable time and effort gathering information.

YOUR DECISION-MAKING STYLE – A MATHEMATICAL APPROACH

If you prefer a more scientific method for identifying your decision-making style, the following procedure may be of interest. If the mere sight of figures turns your brain to jelly (a publisher once warned me that you lose a hundred potential readers for every mathematical formula a book contains), I suggest you turn to the summary at the end of this chapter straight away.

Imagine that an eccentric multi-millionaire offers you a strange choice. Either he will give you a tax-free gift of £1 million or, if you prefer, you can toss a coin; if it comes down heads, he will give you £3 million; if it comes down tails, you get nothing at all. Which will you choose?

If you decide to take the safe £1 million, how would you feel if he now raises the stakes on the coin toss from £3 million to £5 million, or even to £10 million?

Most people, when faced with these options, say they would take the money and run. This is despite the fact that the first gamble has what is termed an 'expected value' of £1.5 million. The expected value is the average outcome of a risk. For example, in a risk with a 50 per cent chance of gaining nothing and a 50 per cent chance of gaining £100, the expected value is £50. This is because you have a 50:50 chance of gaining £100, and half of £100 is £50. Expected value is calculated by multiplying each possible outcome by its value, then adding all the totals together. So, in this example, it would be: 0.5 × £0 + 0.5 × £100 = £50. In the example above, expected value is calculated by multiplying the desired gain (£3 million in this instance) by the probability of winning it, here 50:50 or 0.5 (£3 million × 0.5 = £1.5 million). This means that, if you were to make such a gamble repeatedly, your winnings would be half as large again as your gain had you decided to take the safe £1 million. Even when the second option return is increased to £5 million, the majority of business people will still plump for the safe option.

This may come as a surprise to many who assume that business people will always choose the outcome that offers the richest potential rewards, even when there is an element of risk. An explanation for this behaviour, known as 'cardinal utility theory', was first put forward more than half a century ago by John von Neumann and Oskar Morgenstern in their classic *Theory of Games and Economic Behaviour*.[11] In simple terms, they proposed that, in any risky situation, each of us will have a measurable preference among the available choices; this preference is called our 'utility' and we will choose the alternative which maximizes that utility.

By assigning a numerical value to each preference, it becomes possible to calculate an individual's relationship between utility and reward, known as their 'utility function'. 'Once we know the person's utility function,' says Ralph Swalm, 'the odds he or she assigns to events in a decision-making situation, and the consequences of each possible outcome, we should be able to predict the choice in that situation, since the individual will attempt to maximize his or her utility.'[12]

Decision-Making and Your Risk Preference Profile

The following technique allows you to quantify this response by creating a 'risk preference profile', either of yourself or of anyone else who is prepared to answer three simple questions. This profile will reveal the circumstances under which a high-, medium- or low-risk strategy is preferred. The figures given in the examples below are for illustration only. To produce your own risk profile, you must substitute (a) your own money values, and (b) the different odds involved. From these responses you can plot your own risk preference profile.

QUESTION 1

Imagine you are offered the chance to gamble on the toss of a fair coin. If it comes down heads, you will win a specified sum of money; but if it lands tails, you get nothing. The odds here are 50:50. Alternatively, you can receive £100 with absolutely no risk at all. How much money would you need to be offered to make you choose the gamble over the certain, cash-in-hand £100?

For the moment, assume that a 50:50 gamble with a chance of winning £500 or nothing would just about tempt you away from the certain £100 gift. This gives you two alternatives, a *definite* £100 or a *possible* (50:50 chance of) £500. Both of these options appear equally attractive, and you have no preference for one over the other. The £500 now represents a point of balance between the available options. This is known as your 'Point of Indifference'.

You have to determine your own Point of Indifference for this question and insert the chosen amount into the equation. Maybe you feel that a 50:50 chance of winning £500 or nothing seems too slight for you to give up the cash-in-hand certainty of £100. Perhaps you'd want to raise the stakes to £1,000, or even more. At some amount, however, each option will seem equally attractive, and your Point of Indifference will have been reached.

The next task is to rate the two options on a scale of some kind. Here we will use ratings between −10 (most undesirable choice possible) and +10 (most desirable choice). These ratings, known as 'Preference Values', arc shown on the vertical axis of the profile below.

In this situation we have three outcomes to rate.

1. You win nothing at all. Since you will make neither a profit nor a loss, however, this will be rated at zero.
2. You win £500. This is the best possible outcome and gains a maximum Preference Points rating of +10.
3. Finally, you could gain a certain £100. This is rated midway between 0 and +10, and is allocated 5 Preference Points.

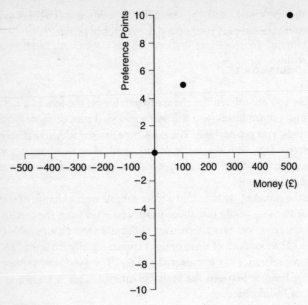

Figure 8.2

These three preference values for £0, £100 and £500 can be plotted on the profile as shown above.

QUESTION 2

Imagine two boxes, Box A and Box B. You have a 50:50 chance of Box A containing either £100 or nothing at all. In Box B there is a cheque whose amount you can write yourself. What is the least value that cheque would need to be for you to prefer Box B to Box A?

If, for instance, the cheque in Box B is for £20, you might decide to take the gamble and open Box A in the hope of gaining the £100, despite the 50:50 risk of it being empty. But would you make the same choice if the cheque in Box B was for £50 . . . or £60?

It is important to choose a sum that genuinely reflects the point at which you become indifferent as to which box you would choose. As with Question 1, the challenge is to identify your Indifference Point, the value at which you have an equal preference for either of the two boxes.

Assume, for the moment, that both boxes will appear equally desirable when the cheque is made out for £80. This amount, or whatever sum you choose, is allocated 2.5 Preference Points, which we can now plot on the profile.

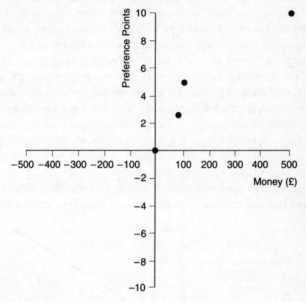

Figure 8.3

Why 2.5 Preference Points?

In this question we are again looking for the 'Point of Indifference' between two amounts. This time the question exploits something we know from the first question: that a certain £100 is worth 5 points; therefore, anything equivalent to half this will be worth 2.5 points: half of 5 points. So the second question asks you what you find equal to an expected value of £50 (2.5 points).

QUESTION 3

In the above two questions there is no risk of your having to pay any money out if your gamble is unsuccessful. In this final question, such a risk is involved. Imagine four playing cards face down on the table. Three are black and one is red. If you pick the red card you will have to pay out a certain amount of money. If you turn over a black card, you will win the same amount as the value of the cheque in the previous question. In our example, this was £80, but you may well have chosen a different amount as representing your Point of Indifference. What is the largest amount of money you would be prepared to risk against a red card turning up, so that you win the amount specified above?

Taking the figure from the example above, you stand to win £80 on any of the three black cards. How much are you prepared to lose on the red card in this 1-in-4 gamble? Let us assume that the maximum amount you are willing to risk is £20. We know that £80 has a preference value of 2.5. The worst outcome in this situation is that you will lose £20. On our rating scale of −10 to 10, this will, therefore, have a negative preference value 10 points less than 2.5, which makes it −7.5 points. By this reckoning, losing £20 is equal to −7.5 preference points.

With this final question answered, we can plot the fifth and final point on our risk preference profile and join them by a smooth line, as

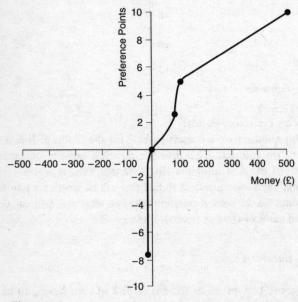

Figure 8.4

illustrated below. This allows you to predict how you – or anyone else for whom you have created a preference profile – will react to risks.

Here's how you do it. First, you use the graph to find the two points that represent the worst and best outcome of the risk. The preference to that risk will be the preference point halfway between these two points. If this preference is greater than the preference to the option whose outcome is certain, then the person will accept the risk. If it is lower than the preference point for the certain option, the person is unlikely to accept it.

Different attitudes towards risk-taking will show specific patterns or signatures on the profiles. Some of these are shown below.

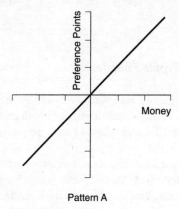

Pattern A

Figure 8.5

Pattern A illustrates the decision-making style of a Gambler as defined above. To this individual, risks are in equal proportion to gains. This is shown by a line that is equally steep in the positive and negative regions of the graph.

Pattern B (see Figure 8.6 overleaf) illustrates the decision-making style of a Fireman who dislikes risks. His or her preference line is steeper in the money-loss region than in the money-gain region.

As an exercise, you might now like to answer the three questions posed above in the style of a Tight-rope Walker and then plot those functions on a graph to see what such a person's preference profile would look like.

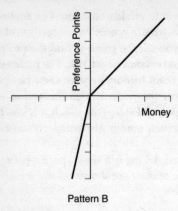

Pattern B

Figure 8.6

How the Preference Profile Functions

Each of the three questions compared a sure outcome to a risky one. The answers allow us to identify the points of indifference at which certainty and risk are seen as equally attractive and when we have no preference for one over the other.

The first question sets our upper limit. It gives us a money value (£500, in the example provided) that represents the top preference point value. Here we have assigned it 10 points. You should note, however, that the rating scale is purely arbitrary, and any range can be selected. All we are doing is choosing a scale that will enable us to make comparisons.

In the second question, the indifference point between two amounts is again being sought. So this question asks what you would regard as equal to an expected value of £50 (2.5 points).

The third question is designed to find a negative value to plot. There are four possible outcomes in this question: three involve profit, one involves loss. The profit is equal to 2.5 preference points. Therefore, in order for the one loss possibility to be equal to the three possibilities for gain, it must be at least as preferable as the sum of the three losses. Therefore, whatever it is, it will equal 2.5 × 3, or −7.5 preference points.

Plotting a Risk Preference Profile is really not as hard as it may appear, and you should quickly get the hang of draughting such profiles and putting them to work. They are well worth the small amount of time and trouble they take to create, since they can provide valuable insights into the different risk-taking attitudes within a decision-making team.

Individuals who are especially wary of taking risks (Firemen) can be identified by a particular pattern on their profile. Here every pound lost will have a higher negative preference than has the same amount gained in positive preference. This means that a loss of £100 might have a preference of −10, while £100 gained would have a preference of only 8. Therefore any risk that involves the possibility of losing money will disproportionately lower a person's preference for that risk.

SUMMARY

In this chapter I have explored some of the factors that profoundly influence our decision-making, especially when handling large volumes of information against deadlines.

- There are three very different decision-making styles, those of the Gambler, the Fireman and the Tight-rope Walker. Each has particular strengths and weaknesses. Identify and be aware of the influence your own style has on the way you make decisions.
- In a group, try to appreciate the way the decision-making styles of other participants may be affecting the choices they propose.
- Time pressures can significantly distort decision-making, causing some people to seek refuge in defensive avoidance, while others go into the panic state of hyper-vigilance. Learn to recognize the causes and consequences of these highly charged emotional states, and work to prevent or reduce the biases they introduce into decision-making.
- There are six traps that lead to poor choices being made. Check any important decisions you are making to ensure that you have avoided all of them.
- By calculating Risk Preference Profiles, you can more accurately predict the course of action an individual is most likely to adopt when making decisions.

In this chapter I have examined some of the psychological background to decision-making and have identified many of the pitfalls. In Chapter Nine I describe a procedure known as 'decision trees'; it will help ensure that the next business decision you take is the best one possible.

9   **Decision-Making with Decision Trees**

'Indecision is somebody who can't say no to anything – a kind
of intellectual nymphomaniac. A lot of smart people just can't
decide what they're going to work on.'

Arno Penzias (Nobel laureate),
quoted in *Fortune* January 1966

In Chapter Eight, I examined some of the ways in which biases, often
subtle and undetected, can adversely affect our ability to make the right
decisions, especially in the face of overload. In this chapter I shall describe
a procedure known as 'Decision Trees', which will help you make clear
and rational business choices even in the face of complex and conflicting
information. This easily mastered approach will enable you to:

- identify all the available options
- discover areas where more information is needed
- quantify various decisions with great accuracy
- make all possible choices explicit, so that every aspect of the task can
  be clearly seen
- decide on the style of decision-making – as a Gambler, Fireman or
  Tight-rope Walker – best suited to the situation.

Far from being a sterile and mechanical process which takes no account
of your intuition and experience, Decision Trees enable you to introduce
your 'gut reactions' into the equation, but in a strictly controlled manner.
This prevents emotions, or hunches based on guesswork, from leading
you into an impulsive and possibly unwise choice.

THE BUILDING BLOCKS OF DECISION-MAKING

All decisions depend on a balance between *desirability* and *probability*. When desirability is high enough, it can override even the lowest probability. The chance of winning a fortune on the UK lottery may be only one in 14 million, but it is rated as so desirable by millions that they return to gamble week after week.

Consider a decision most people make dozens of times each week: when and where to cross a busy street. As you stand watching the traffic speeding past, your brain is calculating the probability of arriving safely at the other side. Only when you are as sure as you can possibly be that it is safe to cross will you launch yourself into the street. The desirability of crossing the street at that particular point will usually be less important than the probability of getting to the other side in one piece. You need to cross over, but exactly where you do so is not usually the overriding consideration.

An occasion may arise, however, when the desirability of crossing the street becomes so overwhelming that you are prepared to risk a far lower probability of arriving safely. Suppose, for example, you have left a baby in its pram on the other side of the street, while you briefly cross the road to make a quick purchase. As you leave the shop, you notice a stranger pushing the pram away. In your frantic attempts to prevent the baby being snatched, you race through the oncoming traffic, risking being knocked down in the process. Your decision to cross at that point and at that moment was determined by the need to save your child.

Because we normally assess desirability and probability with little or no need for conscious thought, there is a strong tendency to use the same approach when making decisions that demand a far more careful evaluation of these two components:

Before making a decision, we must ask two questions:

● How probable is a particular outcome?
● How desirable is that outcome?

In order to answer these questions, you need to ask yourself a number of others:

- Have I examined all the available evidence?
- Have I evaluated it objectively, to avoid falling into some of the traps described in the last chapter?
- Am I being misled by wishful thinking?

You cannot hope to achieve the sort of objective evaluation on which important decisions need to be founded by applying the same everyday approach that helps us to decide trivial issues. Instead, each choice must be objectively assessed in terms of its probability and desirability by creating a decision tree.

To demonstrate how such a tree is constructed, I shall show you how to apply the procedure to one of the most famous of all literary decisions, Hamlet's agonizing over whether it was better 'To be or not to be . . .'[1] The two options that Hamlet saw open to him, following the marriage of his mother to the man he suspected of murdering his father, were stark. Should he carry on living or take his own life? These alternatives can be pictured as branches from a single stem:

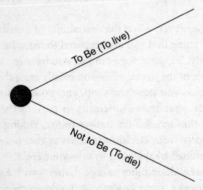

Figure 9.1 *'Hamlet's choice'*

For either course of action there will clearly be one or more consequences, and the next stage in developing the tree is to write down the consequences of each choice. In his soliloquy, Hamlet describes these as either to live and suffer 'The slings and arrows of outrageous fortune' or to die and risk being tormented by dreams: 'For in that sleep of death what dreams may come . . .'

Hamlet's expanded decision tree now looks like this:

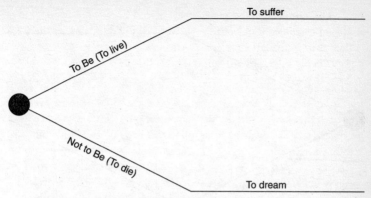

Figure 9.2 *'Hamlet's expanded decision tree'*

But the Prince of Denmark was also of the opinion that he might discover, in death, the peace of mind he was denied in life:

> 'To die, to sleep –
> No more; and by a sleep to say we end
> The heart-ache and the thousand natural shocks
> That flesh is heir to. 'Tis a consummation
> Devoutly to be wish'd.'

This additional consequence of dying is added to the tree, completing the structure (see Figure 9.3, overleaf).

Hamlet's decision tree includes all the outcomes that he seemingly took into account when deciding whether or not to end his life with a 'bare bodkin'. Because the range of choices made available to him by Shakespeare was limited, the final Tree is simpler than those normally found when analysing a complex decision.

The next step is to show how each of the outcomes we have identified can be evaluated in terms of their desirability and probability.

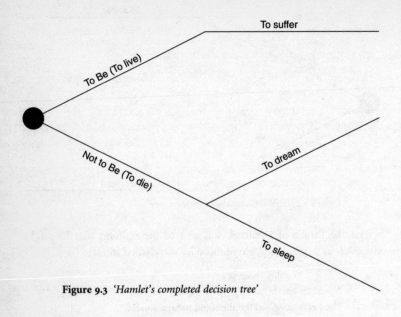

Figure 9.3 *'Hamlet's completed decision tree'*

ASSESSING DESIRABILITY

Decisions produce outcomes that are, in varying degrees, desirable or undesirable. These can be evaluated by assigning each one a numerical value. Outcomes we dislike are rated using negative values, while desirable consequences have positive values.

In their landmark paper on decision analysis, Desmond Graves and David Lethbridge, of the Oxford Centre for Management Studies, suggest a range extending from +6 (most desirable outcome) to −6 (least desirable consequence). Had this system been around in the court of King Claudius, how might Hamlet have assessed the desirability, or otherwise, of the options available to him?

He clearly considered 'dreamless death' as the best possible outcome one could hope for, viewing it as: 'a consummation devoutly to be wish'd'. This strongly suggests he would have assigned it a desirability rating of +6.

What stopped him from immediate suicide was the terror that his sleep of death might be disturbed by hideous and unending dreams:

> 'For in that sleep of death what dreams may come,
> When we have shuffled off this mortal coil,
> Must give us pause.'

Since Hamlet seems to look on this as a fate worse than death and an outcome to be avoided at all costs, he would probably have rated it as −6.

He also appeared to regard living and suffering as preferable to dying and dreaming:

> 'But that the dread of something after death –
> The undiscover'd country, from whose bourn
> No traveller returns – puzzles the will,
> And makes us rather bear those ills we have
> Than fly to others that we know not of?
> Thus conscience does make cowards of us all.'

Living and suffering was, however, less desirable than sleepless death:

> 'To die, to sleep –
> No more; and by a sleep to say we end
> The heart-ache and the thousand natural shocks
> That flesh is heir to. 'Tis a consummation
> Devoutly to be wish'd.'

Assessing these two outcomes, he might have given 'living and suffering' a rating of −3, indicating a moderate level of dislike.

Bringing these ratings together, we can now produce a Desirability Table that lists all the consequences Hamlet foresaw stemming from his life-or-death decision:

Options	Consequences	Desirability
To be	To suffer	−3
Not to be	To have terrible dreams	−6
	To enjoy dreamless sleep	+6

With the desirability of these possible outcomes established, we can now explore how likely each one appears to be.

ASSESSING PROBABILITY

Since – apart from death and taxes – it is rarely possible to know exactly how likely a particular outcome will be, all one can do is make an educated guess as to its probability. The method most widely used for rating probability is to use a scale from 0 (it can never happen) to 1 (it will certainly happen). If there is a 50:50 chance of something happening, it is given a rating of 0.5.

Employing this rating scale on Hamlet's decision tree, we see that he considered that living could produce only one outcome: continued suffering from the 'slings and arrows of outrageous fortune'. As he was certain of this consequence, it is given a probability rating of 1. When contemplating suicide, Hamlet had to weigh the probability of dreamless sleep against the likelihood of perpetual torment. It seems he felt each was equally probable, giving both of these outcomes a rating of 0.5.

A table showing the desirability and probability for each of the three consequences given above looks like this:

Options	Consequences	Desirability	Probability
To be	To suffer	−3	1
Not to be	To have terrible dreams	−6	0.5
	To enjoy dreamless sleep	+6	0.5

Had Hamlet viewed his past life more favourably, and had he believed his behaviour to have been virtuous, he might well have rated his chances of escaping nightmares throughout eternity more highly, in which case the probability of this consequence could have dropped from 0.5 to 0.3 or even lower.

Because the total of all scores for all the outcomes resulting from a single course of action must always equal 1, reducing the probability of tormenting dreams from 0.5 to 0.3 increases the probability of 'dreamless death' from 0.5 to 0.7. His final comment, 'Thus conscience does make cowards of us all,' strongly suggests, however, that he felt incapable of adopting anything but the most pessimistic view of his chances.

With desirability and probability ratings established, the best course of action can now be obtained by the simple expedient of multiplying the two together to produce a Decision Value. The higher this value, the wiser it would be to adopt this course of action.

Options	Consequences	Desirability × Probability		Decision Value
To be (to live)	To suffer	−3	1	−3
Not to be (to die)	To dream	−6	0.5	−3
	To sleep	+6	0.5	+3

From this table, it is clear that Hamlet's most logical course of action would have been to kill himself! The worst fate awaiting him after death is to dream throughout all eternity (−6), but this turns out to be no worse than carrying on living and suffering because, while the desirability of this consequence is greater (−3), its far higher probability (1) means it has exactly the same Decision Value (−3).

Bear in mind that we are dealing here with subjective impressions of the desirability and probability of each consequence. Hamlet seems to have been very strongly of the view that bad dreams and dreamless sleep were equally likely after committing suicide. Because of this and far greater desirability of dreamless sleep (+6), suicide obtains the highest Decision Value and therefore most desirable course of action.

There is, of course, a fourth possible outcome: to go on living, but without suffering. Since Hamlet did not take his own life, he must have entertained such hopes, only Shakespeare never bothered to tell his audience. But the notion that Hamlet withheld some of his thoughts on the matter is consistent with modern research, according to which we often decide on the basis of beliefs, feelings and opinions that we are either unwilling or unable to share with others.

When constructing the branches of your decision tree, try to come up with as many courses of action as possible. Aim to have at least four options per tree, even if one or two seem unrealistic and impractical. By widening your range of possibilities, it becomes easier to put all the viable outcomes into perspective.

DECISION TREES IN BUSINESS

The tree we are going to construct now is considerably more complicated than the one for Hamlet. As we work through its development together, however, you will find this ordered approach resolves any confusions and biases resulting from information overload. Exactly the same approach can be used when making all decisions in your professional or personal life.

Don's Dilemma

Don Ellis is sales director of an import–export company dealing with electronic games. Recently he bought a large number of electronic games, only to find they went out of fashion faster than he had anticipated. As a result he now has a warehouse filled with expensive stock which he has to shift in the run-up to Christmas. His only hope of doing so is to sell in bulk to one of two large retail outlets.

Don knows both their chief buyers personally and feels confident he can persuade one of them to help him out. But he knows that whichever chain agrees to take the game will want to sell it exclusively.

The chief buyer for Company A is Alison Martin. She was Don's first choice because her stores are located in prosperous neighbourhoods where sales of similarly high-priced and sophisticated games have historically been strong. He believes Alison's retail outlets are capable of moving more of the product for him in a shorter period of time than the retail outlets of Company B.

This knowledge must be set against the fact that he is on better terms with the chief buyer for Company B, an amiable individual called Alan Peters, with whom he regularly plays golf.

Don knows he will have to tread very carefully in his negotiations, since Alison and Alan are deadly rivals. By offering his game to one of them, he greatly reduces the likelihood that the other will show any interest, should his initial negotiations fall through. 'I think I could make the best deal with Alison because her store would promote the line hard, they have a good track record with my company and are more likely to re-order, provided the original deal proves successful,' Don muses. 'Against this, Alan is more likely to take the goods, even though his first order will be smaller. But if his sales are poor – which they could well be, due to his outlets being less suitable for selling this type of merchandise – he is unlikely to re-order.

'I have made some good deals with Alison in the past, and it is just possible that, if I go to Alan first and get turned down, she might still be prepared to do business with me. On the other hand, Alan dislikes Alison so intensely that, if I go to her first and get nowhere, it is unlikely I will be able to go back to him and secure a contract, despite our friendship. He's bound to feel let down by my not approaching him right away.

'If I make the wrong decision and fail to sell to either of them, I shall have a tough job getting rid of my stock. There are no other outlets large and specialized enough to take the product in the quantity I have available. The company will stand to lose a lot of money, and my job could be in jeopardy for having over-ordered the line in the first place. I must make a deal with either Alison or Alan. But how can I decide which one to approach first?'

This is typical of the kind of decision confronting business people daily, combining as it does uncertainty and risk. Here's how constructing a decision tree can help Don out.

He starts by giving the three options available to him a Desirability Rating:

Options	Desirability
Sell to Alan	+5
Sell to Alison	+6
Sell to neither	−6

Don's next task is to evaluate the probability of acceptance or rejection of the deal by each of his two buyers. This requires careful thought but, based on his past knowledge and experience of dealing with the two buyers, he assigns these values as below.

Options	Probability		
First Choice	Accept	Reject	Total
Approach Alan	0.7	0.3	1
Approach Alison	0.6	0.4	1

(The probability ratings for each outcome with an option must always total 1.)

Finally, Don must work out his chances of persuading either Alison or Alan to buy his goods when each knows the other has already turned him down. Again, he has to make an educated guess based on his knowledge of their individual personalities.

Options	Probability		
Second Choice	Accept	Reject	Total
Approach Alan	0.2	0.8	1
Approach Alison	0.3	0.7	1

With values for desirability and probability assigned, Don now constructs the decision tree illustrated opposite and writes in his ratings. The structure of this tree is more extensive than the one we created earlier because Don, unlike Hamlet, could be faced with a second choice if his first approach to either Alison or Alan proves unsuccessful.

To obtain the final probability rating of the outcome of these second approaches, all Don has to do is carry out some simple arithmetic. Consider, for example, the chances of his failing to make any sale at all because, having first been turned down by Alan, his approach is spurned by an angry Alison (an outcome depicted in the top branch of the decision tree). The probability of this happening is obtained by multiplying the probability of a rejection by Alan (0.3) by the probability of a subsequent refusal to buy from Alison (0.7). This calculation is written on the top line of the tree under the probability heading.

Don then calculates the probability of Alan refusing to do business with him after Alison has turned him down as 0.4 (the probability of

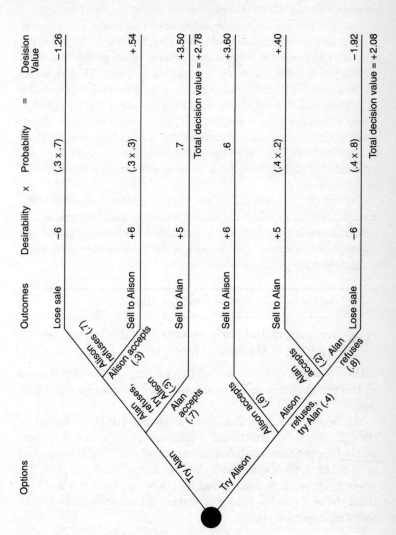

Figure 9.4 'Alan/Alison decision tree'

Alison refusing) times 0.8 (the probability of Alan refusing, if asked second). This calculation is written on the lowest branch of the tree.

Don now turns to the happier outcome of a successful sale, either at the first attempt or after an initial refusal by either buyer. The arithmetic is so straightforward if either Alison or Alan agrees to the deal when approached first that you can easily work it out for yourself. If Alan rejects the deal (0.6) but then Alison agrees to buy (0.3), the probability of Don extricating himself from his awkward situation and selling his games to Alison's company is 0.6 × 0.3. Similarly, given the probability of Alison turning him down when approached first (0.4) and the probability of Alan giving him a contract if approached second (0.2), we get an overall probability of Alan agreeing to do business with him as a second choice of 0.4 × 0.2.

Once all the probabilities have been filled in on the six branches of the tree, Don can easily calculate Decision Values for each outcome within a particular option by simply multiplying desirability by overall probability and then adding up the totals for each of the two choices open to him. These give the following values:

Option	Decision Value
Try selling to Alan first	$(-1.26) + (+0.54) + (+3.5) = 2.78$
Try selling to Alison first	$(+3.6) + (+0.4) + (-1.92) = 2.08$

On the basis of this decision tree, Don's best tactic is to offer the toys to Alan first, even though his initial impulse had been to approach Alison first.

It is, of course, impossible to know in advance that Don's decision is the right one. It may well be that Alison would have agreed to the deal and so done well for him, while Alan may not reject the deal if approached second. Life is full of uncertainties and imponderables. By adopting this scientific approach to making decisions, however, both you and Don stand the best possible chance of making the wisest decision for the following important reasons.

1. The task of fixing number values to each element in decision-making focuses your attention on specific issues and prevents you from being distracted by more general and less essential aspects of the situation. This

is especially valuable when making decisions in the face of information overload.

2. Constructing decision trees enables you to make explicit all possible options and outcomes. By writing them down on paper you ensure that nothing is overlooked or forgotten, again a vital consideration when working under pressure of time and large volumes of information.

As I explained in Chapter Six, short-term memory has a strictly limited capacity and, once that upper limit is exceeded, important facts will be forgotten. When the brain is already approaching its upper limits for data processing, confusion and forgetfulness become highly probable. As a result, decisions may be made following an incomplete consideration of all the information available.

3. When constructing your decision tree you will be stimulating the flow of ideas and as a result may well discover new courses of action.

4. Less obvious options, which might otherwise have been overlooked, will spring to mind far more readily than when you are thinking about available choices in an unstructured manner.

5. While a decision tree allows you to take account of personal preferences, your hunches, intuitions and emotional response to a situation, it keeps that situation under control. There is far less risk of your becoming overwhelmed by your feelings.

6. Assigning numbers to the desirability and probability of outcomes does not eliminate spontaneity from decision-making, but it does increase your confidence in making objective rather than subjective choices.

I cannot deny that taking a guess, or tossing a coin, is a faster way of making decisions. When faced with deadlines and information overload, the temptation for just such a 'quick fix' is extremely powerful. This is especially so if your decision-making style is that of the risk-taking Gambler.

SUMMARY

Whenever you have an important decision to make, one on which your own or your company's success depends, it will pay to analyse your options as objectively as possible.

- Assess how your own decision-making style, as well as those of any others involved in the process, may be influencing your choices.
- Calculate the probability and desirability of as many outcomes as possible, then construct a decision tree to make these relationships explicit.

Once you have had some practice with constructing such trees and calculating Decision Values, you will find the procedure fast, easy and effective.

As I said at the start of this chapter, decision trees allow you to cut through the confusion created by information overload, evaluate all possible outcomes objectively and arrive at a sound judgement of the most favourable option open to you.

> 'The office environment is in general free from the hazards of
> the factory, but it can cause or contribute to ill health and
> accidents, in both obvious and more subtle ways.'
>
> Dr David J. Murray-Bruce, *Promoting Employee Health*

So far in this book I have been looking at various strategies and procedures
for easing the burden of information overload. In this chapter I want
first to consider the likely effects of the surroundings in which the daily
challenge of overload is dealt with, and then to suggest practical ways in
which you can improve mental and physical health.

The importance of a healthy workplace was brought home to me a
couple of years ago when I was invited to tour the recently opened office
of an international computer company. It was an impressive sight and I
was impressed. The air was warm and dry, filled with the gentle hum of
laser-printers, photocopiers and fax machines. Although there were
large windows on three sides of the room, little sunshine could penetrate
their deeply tinted glass. In the subdued lighting, computer screens
flickered through a cavernous vastness. The synthetic fabric of upholstery,
curtains and carpets was all carefully colour co-ordinated. Clearly, no
expense had been spared to create a gleaming icon of corporate power
and prestige.

As I said, the office impressed me – but not in the way the designers
had intended. What struck me most forcibly was the potential of this
workplace to increase the risks posed by information overload.

Eighteen months later, I found my initial concerns were justified:
managers reported high levels of absenteeism and numerous complaints

of minor health problems, distressing to sufferers and detrimental to productivity.

Does your own office pose similar hazards? Complete the following check-list and find out:

Rate your workplace by ticking whichever of these statements apply.

1. The view from my desk consists of (a) green spaces (i.e. country-side, park, gardens, etc.); (b) urban scenery (i.e. other offices, houses, streets, etc.); (c) I have no view at all.
2. The office where I work has (a) an oasis of green plants within sight of my desk; (b) greenery out of sight of my desk; (c) no real greenery, except for an occasional pot plant.
3. My work area is illuminated (a) mainly by natural light; (b) by a mixture of natural and artificial light; (c) entirely by artificial light.
4. There are fax machines, laser-printers, photocopiers, etc. (a) in a different room from the one I work in; (b) in the same room, but at some distance from my desk; (c) close to my desk.
5. My workplace is ventilated by (a) opening a window; (b) air conditioning.
6. My workplace is centrally heated: (a) no; (b) partly; (c) entirely.
7. The noise levels in my office are: (a) low; (b) moderately high; (c) very high.
8. People in my office seem to go down with colds and flu-like illnesses (a) less often than people working in other offices; (b) with about the same frequency; (c) more frequently.
9. At the end of the working day I have a headache (a) seldom; (b) fairly often; (c) frequently.
10. At the end of the working day, my nose and sinuses feel stuffed up (a) seldom; (b) fairly often; (c) frequently.

Score 1 point for each (a) response ticked, 2 for each (b) and three for each (c).

How Sick Is Your Office?

10–15: No cause for concern. You are fortunate to work in surroundings that safeguard your health.

16–20: There are some risks in your present working environment. Check the comments below concerning different sources of ill-health, and take the necessary steps to correct the problem.

21–25: Your office does not seem to be a very healthy place in which to work, and it is likely to exacerbate the dangers of information overload. Take prompt steps to remedy those aspects of the environment that are within your powers to change.

26+: Your working environment poses a significant threat to physical well-being and will certainly make it far harder for you to cope with the pressures of information overload. It is important that you make whatever changes are within your power and that you recognize the extent to which these surroundings may be contributing to any health problems from which you or your colleagues have suffered.

Let's start by considering one of the most widespread, yet easily remedied, health problems found in the great majority of modern offices.

DEHYDRATION

The notion that people who work in modern, centrally heated, air-conditioned offices and with unlimited access to liquids of all kinds could become dehydrated may seem absurd. Yet research suggests that a majority of desk workers regularly suffer a level of dehydration sufficient to impair their performance and increase the risk of Information Fatigue Syndrome (IFS).

We lose water continually, through the actions of our kidneys and evaporation from skin and lungs. Unfortunately we start to feel thirsty only when our mouth grows dry through lack of saliva. By this time, however, our body has become sufficiently dehydrated to trigger changes that are detrimental to our health. This is especially true for adults, whose thirst-sensation is less acute than in people under the age of twenty.[1] An already bad situation is then often made worse, because a busy, preoccupied, individual may continue to ignore his or her body's increasingly urgent clamour for liquid.

The usual workplace remedies for thirst – tea, coffee, cola drinks or alcohol – only make the situation worse. All are potent diuretics, which is to say they encourage the production of urine. By quenching your thirst in this way, you end up flushing more fluid out of the body than you have just taken in. As a result, the more frequently you 'refresh' yourself with cups of tea, coffee or colas, the more rapidly you will dehydrate. Nor is the lunch-time alcoholic drink, however refreshed you may feel initially, any more beneficial.

The reason why your thirst immediately disappears after you have a drink has nothing to do with the body being instantly rehydrated. In fact it takes from thirty to sixty minutes for all the liquid to be absorbed into the body fluids. It is the distension of the stomach and other portions of the upper digestive tract that temporarily turns off the thirst centre in the brain. This mechanism helps protect the body against taking in too much fluid at any one time. As one medical authority points out: 'Were his thirst sensation not temporarily relieved after drinking of water, he would continue to drink more and more. When all this water should finally become absorbed, his body fluids would be far more diluted than normal, and he would have created an abnormal condition opposite to that which he was attempting to correct.'[2] Exactly the same relief of thirst, for between five and thirty minutes, has been achieved in experiments by passing a balloon into the stomach of volunteers and then inflating it!

Low relative humidity (moisture content of the air) in many centrally heated, air-conditioned, high-tech offices makes them extremely de-hydrating places in which to work. Comfortable surroundings, which will help reduce the risk of IFS, are a temperature of 20°C (68°F) and a relative humidity of between 50 per cent and 55 per cent. In some offices, I have measured moisture levels as low as 20 per cent, a relative humidity similar to that found in the Sahara desert!

Frequent fliers may also like to note that the cabins of long-haul jets tend to be even more dehydrating, with a moisture content well below 10 per cent, in some instances as low as 1 per cent.[3] This puts executives who regularly fly long distance between air-conditioned offices in double-dehydration jeopardy.

'Dehydration occurs commonly although most people aren't aware of some of the subtle signs,' comments travel writer Diana Fairechild. 'Normally we exhale approximately 20 per cent of our water intake.

Aboard long-haul flights this figure will rise to almost 50 per cent.'[4] As a further illustration of how low relative humidity can be in aircraft, medical advice to aircrew is to drink 250 millilitres of water per *hour* of flight time.

Even when the relative humidity is a comfortable 50 per cent, you are therefore still likely to be losing water at a rapid rate. The answer is simple and well within anyone's power to correct. All you need do is drink more water!

Drink Eight Glasses a Day

If you believe water is strictly for swimming or bathing in, you may find my suggestion that you drink 250 ml (just under half a pint) of water eight times a day hard to swallow. If so, perhaps the following health benefits will persuade you. (While the advice to drink more water is generally sound, do not do so without seeking medical advice if you have kidney or heart disease, are receiving vasopressin therapy, or are a male with a prostate condition.) By drinking this amount of water daily:

● You will boost your physical endurance by causing muscles to burn less glycogen (used to provide energy) when engaging in demanding activities.

● It will help you avoid common infections. Lining your nasal passages and sinuses is a sticky mucus containing antibodies to trap and destroy invading germs; this protects you against common ailments such as colds and flu. Even a small amount of dehydration can cause this mucus to dry up, allowing germs to gain access more easily. This is likely to happen if you work in an office with a relative humidity of less than 40 per cent.[5]

● It will prevent constipation. This is a common problem for sedentary workers whose lack of exercise makes it harder for food to pass through their digestive system. Lack of water can also cause, or aggravate, this health problem. Even if you have very soft stools or diarrhoea, this is no reason for cutting down on your water intake; all this means is that insufficient water is being absorbed from your last meal as it moved through the digestive tract, and this, in turn, speeds dehydration.

● It will significantly reduce the risk of developing kidney stones. Diluting your urine helps prevent the formation of salt crystals that can lead to these agonizing stones. (Incidentally, a sure sign that your body has become significantly dehydrated is dark yellow urine. Try to ensure that it remains very pale or even colourless. This is especially important when visiting countries with a far higher outside temperature than the one to which you are accustomed.)

● It will enhance your powers of concentration and reaction time, helping you make faster and better decisions. This occurs because your whole body is working more comfortably and efficiently. Even minor dehydration imposes stresses on the body and when water loss becomes more severe it can cause significant difficulties for the entire system.

Sip your eight glasses a day slowly; never be tempted to gulp it all down in one go. I suggest keeping a bottle of (preferably iced) water on your desk, in your briefcase, at home and in your car. My own preferred container is a plastic bottle designed for use on small boats. This has a twist top which, when turned, causes a drinking straw to protrude. When twisted in the opposite direction the bottle is sealed and cannot spill.

One objection sometimes raised when I suggest this simple, no-cost way of improving health while reducing stress and the risk of IFS is that it makes trips to the lavatory more frequent. While true, this is surely a small price to pay for so many benefits. Anyway, the walk to the nearest convenience provides a much-needed break from sitting at your desk.

A final point about water – and this applies to drinking any liquid – avoid drinking a large amount just before a meal since, by diluting the stomach acid, it can impair your digestion. Such a hazard is avoided by following my suggestion of sipping the water over the entire working day.

OFFICE AIR – THE ION FACTOR

Computers, laser-printers, fax machines, and the synthetic fabrics found in the majority of offices lead to the production of positive ions. Clothes and furnishings made from synthetic fibres only worsen matters because, being non-conductors, they trap electrical charges, causing static electricity. When such material holds a positive charge, it draws the health-giving negative ions from the atmosphere, reducing the numbers available to be inhaled.

Positively charged ions have been shown to increase stress, slow mental responses and make people feel irritable and edgy. They are plentiful immediately before thunderstorms, as well as being present in the mistral winds of southern Europe and the Santa Ana – Witches Wind – of southern California, and are well known to trigger marked changes in mood.

When inhaled, positive ions increase the level of a neurotransmitter called serotonin in brain and body tissues. This powerful substance has been called the 'ultimate downer' because, as levels rise, people become increasingly tense, irritable, tired and depressed. Associated with these emotional changes are physical problems such as aching joints, insomnia, migraines and difficulty in breathing. A marked rise in positive ions has even been linked with rising crime.[6]

By contrast, when serotonin levels fall we become happier, more optimistic and relaxed; our brains work more efficiently, we enjoy better sleep, and sensations of pain are reduced. This fall in serotonin can be produced by the presence of negative ions in the atmosphere.

Negative ions are produced naturally by rain, waterfalls, waves and wide expanses of water – one reason why people find it so much easier to relax on the beach or at the lakeside.

The easiest way to create a constant flow of negative ions in your work area is by the use of a commercial ionizer. These small, inexpensive devices can be placed on the desk or in your general working area. One of the best I have come across in my researches is the Elanra,[7] designed and built in Australia.

If possible, wear clothes made from natural fibres – linen, cotton, silk or wool – and surround yourself with curtains, carpets and upholstery made from the same materials.

THE HEALING POWER OF SUNLIGHT

Many office workers these days spend a great part – if not all – of their time working by artificial light; this is, typically, one of two types, neither of which has a spectrum anything like that of natural light. Compared with sunlight, tungsten bulbs produce a far higher proportion of red light. The other popular type of office lighting, cool white fluorescent tubes, produces far more green than is found in natural daylight.

Research suggests that, because for millions of years we have been exposed to only natural light – the first electric bulb flickered into life only in 1879 – long-term exposure to artificial light with its very different spectrum can cause physical and mental stress. In my regular consultations with major European and US corporations I have often suggested that great benefits to health, morale and performance can be achieved by ensuring that all the lights used are as close as possible to natural light.

For a desk lamp, buy a bulb designed for use by artists or designers who require natural light for their work. This type of bulb has a blue tinge to it and can be found in shops selling artists' materials, electrical goods and suppliers' stores that cater for people who knit or sew. In offices, I suggest that any cool white fluorescent tubes be replaced by daylight-corrected ones.

An even better option, of course, is to work by natural daylight as much as possible. Unfortunately the design of many large, open-plan offices means that many employees work far from the windows, and the amount of natural light is often limited by blinds or tinted glass.

LEVELS OF ILLUMINATION

Before leaving this topic, attention should also be paid to the level of the illumination by which you are reading or doing similar close work. While it is unlikely to do actual damage to your eyes by working in the wrong kind of light, it can cause eye fatigue, so impairing performance. By the 'wrong kind' of light I mean not only lighting that is too dim to easily see by, but also glaring, overly bright or haphazard illumination.

The output of a light source is measured in 'lumens' and the resulting illumination in 'lux'. To give an idea of the levels found on a bright but not sunny day, you might measure 5,000 lux. Close the window, and it may fall by half. In cricket, play will be stopped due to 'bad light' when the level falls to 100 lux. In some of the offices I have inspected, including the high-tech one described at the beginning of this chapter, levels have been as low as 200 lux.

While the efficiency of the eye improves as the light increases, up to daylight level, people's preferences vary greatly, ranging from 1,000 lux down to 400 lux. Studies suggest that a majority of workers prefer 500 lux, a level recommended by the standard reference for lighting engineers, *The Illuminating Engineering Society (IES) Code for Interior Lighting.*

In his book *Promoting Employee Health*,[8] Dr David J. Murray-Bruce, Group Senior Medical Officer for National Westminster Bank plc, advises the following levels: general office 500 lux, typing and machine areas 750 lux, filing areas 300 lux.

When general levels of illumination have to be kept low in order to prevent reflections from computer monitors, a desk lamp should be provided for each worker. Glare can be prevented by such simple expedients as adding shades, improving diffusers, raising the level of light fittings, or even by directing them towards the ceiling and working by reflected light.

The eye quickly becomes fatigued by flickering light such as is produced by a faulty fluorescent tube – even when this is tolerated or even goes unnoticed by preoccupied workers.

Lengthy periods spent working on a computer screen, with the gaze fixed at a certain distance, tires the ciliary muscles which focus the lens of the eye, making them feel heavy and uncomfortable. Counter this by breaking off from work once every twenty minutes or so and gazing into the distance. This will help the ciliary muscles relax. Simple exercises, such as moving a raised finger across your field of vision and following it with your eyes, can also help to prevent fatigue.

GREENERY SCENERY

'Nature matters to people', claims Dr Rachel Kaplan[9] from the School of Natural Resources, University of Michigan, Ann Arbor. 'Big trees and small trees, glistening water, chirping birds, budding bushes, and colourful flowers – these are important ingredients in a good life. To have these available only rarely, when and if one can afford to leave the city, deprives people of tranquillity and spiritual sustenance.'

Studies have shown that natural views in the workplace can lower levels of stress and increase job satisfaction. Workers who can see grass, trees and flowers through their office windows report feeling less stressful and are more satisfied than those who can see only buildings or who have no outside view. The former also make fewer complaints of having headaches, sore eyes, aching muscles and similar minor ailments. In one study, which measured brain activity, subjects were found to be more 'wakefully relaxed' when they looked at plants and flowers than when faced by an urban landscape.[10] There is, for example, a fall in blood pressure among volunteers located in natural surroundings. This is important, since an increase in the pumping (systolic pressure) of the heart has been linked to hostile, tense and depressed moods.[11] For most people, natural scenery has the additional advantage of arousing positive and pleasurable feelings.

While we can hardly import trees, water and chirping birds into the average office, having some contact with nature by having various types of pot plants near by can do much to reduce the risk of stress caused by overload among managers. It is even more beneficial to have an office with views across natural surroundings, or to spend some time each day in a park or the countryside. Even fifteen minutes spent strolling among trees and bushes lifts the spirits and improve one's sense of well-being.

THE STRESSFUL BREATH

There is another factor in the way we work that can increase our risk of stress in general and of IFS in particular; it has to do with the way we breathe when sitting at a computer or hunched over a desk. In such a position, we have a tendency to take shorter, shallower breaths, reaching only the middle area of the lungs, rather than deep, full breaths, which draw the air down to the lower portions where the exchange of oxygen and carbon dioxide is most efficient. Since breathing is normally a subconscious activity, we can be unaware that anything untoward is happening, until we find our concentration faltering and a headache developing.

When your breathing is restricted and inefficient, your stress levels quickly rise. When your breathing is full and efficient, your whole system, emotional, physical and intellectual, is enhanced. This is why we describe somebody who is filled with creative life and energy as being 'inspired' or having an 'inspiration'. By learning to pay attention to this essential and mainly automatic process, which is performed between 16,000 and 20,000 times a day, you will be able to remove much needless tension from your body and enable your brain to function more easily and efficiently.

Stop reading for a moment and consider how you are sitting or lying while reading this book. If you are at a desk, perhaps you are leaning forward and taking the weight of your upper body on your arms and shoulders. If you are lying down, perhaps your back and shoulders are propped up on pillows. In either case, it is unlikely that your current posture is helping you to breathe efficiently.

For rhythmical abdominal breathing, your weight should be evenly distributed: through the spine and pelvis when you are seated, and through the spine and legs when standing. This balance is frequently not practised by desk-bound workers and, as a direct result, their breathing is adversely affected. For instance, if your weight is taken on your shoulders and elbows, as often happens when somebody is leaning forward over a desk, the shoulder muscles tense and become involved in the breathing process.

By forcing the abdominal organs upwards, this hunched sitting position also restricts the diaphragm and limits the outward movement of the lower ribs. Where poor posture has become a habit, efficient lung and rib-cage expansion are chronically restricted, so reducing the ability to deal with stressful situations.

Emotions, especially those that get bottled up, also exert a profound effect on the way we breathe, especially if great self-control is required to keep them suppressed. Whenever we fight to conceal a strong emotion, such as anger or fear, the diaphragm and the abdominal muscles tense, drawing the breastbone and rib-cage downwards. To take a breath under these conditions, our shoulder and neck muscles are forced to work harder so as to overcome the downward force. This produces fast, shallow breathing and a condition called *hyperventilation*. Smokers in particular are at risk because they draw air into their lungs with a sucking motion, using face, throat and upper-limb muscles rather than the diaphragm.

HYPERVENTILATION AND THE STRESS RESPONSE

One of the first things to happen when we become stressed is that the rate (breaths per minute) and type of our breathing changes. It may increase from between twelve and sixteen (which is normal) to thirty or more, as occurs during panic attacks. At the same time, our breathing becomes shallower and less efficient because only the upper portions of the lungs are involved.

The range and variety of distressing effects caused by even a minor increase in our rate of breathing are seldom fully appreciated. They include:

- rapidly beating heart
- dizziness (especially in younger people)
- anxiety and panic attacks
- an inability to concentrate
- disturbed sleep and/or nightmares
- increased sweating under the armpits and on the palms (emotional sweating).

All these damaging effects are due to faulty breathing creating an imbalance in the ratio of carbon dioxide and oxygen in the bloodstream. This triggers an increase in the activity of nerve cells, while, at the same time, the veins constrict, reducing the oxygen supply to the brain, causing it to function more sluggishly.

Test Your Breathing

Place one hand on your chest and the other on your stomach. Breathe normally for a while and notice which hand rises the most. If your lower hand moves further each time you breathe in and out, then you are breathing abdominally by raising and lowering a broad dome-shaped muscle called the diaphragm. If your upper hand moves more, then you are breathing in and out by expanding and reducing your chest cavity by means of the muscles between your ribs. This is known as chest or 'costal' breathing. To see how these two forms of breathing affect us, we need to take a look at the mechanisms involved.

Place the fingers of both hands along the lower edge of your ribs, beginning in the middle where they meet at the breastbone (or sternum). Applying gentle pressure with your fingertips, distinguish the firmness of the rib-cage from the softness of your abdomen. Follow the ribs round towards your spine. At your back, the ribs are more difficult to detect due to strong bands of muscles, so apply firmer pressure. What you can feel is your diaphragm. Three vital structures, the food pipe (oesophagus) and two major blood vessels (vena cava and aorta), pass through the diaphragm. As a result, it plays an important role in your digestion and blood circulation. A strong diaphragm can help prevent stomach acid passing back into the oesophagus, causing heartburn, and it helps blood flowing back from your legs, abdomen and pelvis to reach the heart.

The flattening and contracting of the diaphragm increases abdominal pressure and this, together with the abdominal muscles, creates an inflatable jacket for supporting the low back. As the diaphragm contracts and flattens, the volume of your thorax increases, drawing air into the lungs. Your chest size is also increased through the action of muscles which lift the upper ribs and sternum forward and upwards.

Chest (costal) breathing is characterized by an outward and upward movement of the rib-cage using the intercostal muscles, which are located between each rib. Because this expansion is focused on the midpoint of the chest, it is the middle of the lungs that receives the most oxygen; unfortunately, it is the lower parts of the lungs that are richest in blood. This means that chest breathing is less efficient during resting periods, requiring more work to achieve the same amount of blood gas mixing.

The harder your body has to work, the more oxygen it needs and the greater the number of breaths you must take. Chest breathing is useful during vigorous exercise but inappropriate for everyday activities.

Because it forms part of the fight–flight response, costal breathing occurs when we are aroused by an external or internal threat; as a result, it is associated with other stress symptoms, such as tension and anxiety. This means that chest breathing performed during a rest period can lead to feelings of tension and anxiety.

Paradoxical breathing occurs when both the diaphragm and the abdominal muscles are contracted at the same time, as if the person were preparing to receive a blow. This could protect against a genuine attack by turning the muscle into a rigid wall. When it occurs as a stress response, however, inhalation becomes weak and inefficient.

Breathing Away Stress

Here are three simple exercises that will help you to breathe away stress by allowing your body to inhale and exhale in an efficient and relaxed manner.

ABDOMINAL BREATHING

Try to remember to make regular checks on your posture, especially when working for long periods at a computer terminal or over a desk. By doing so you will significantly improve your ability to cope with stressful challenges – as well as sparing yourself the discomfort of many muscular aches and pains.

Sit as upright as possible, with your lower back (lumbar region) well supported. If your chair fails to provide such support, change it for one that does. Failing that, place a small pillow behind your lower back. When you are sitting upright your spine provides proper support to your head without placing your muscles under needless tension. Also, the air is able to flow smoothly and freely into your lungs. Keep your legs uncrossed and support your feet on a rest. These two simple actions will prevent strain to the muscles of your legs, pelvis and lower back, as well as improving your circulation.

When you are sitting comfortably upright, close your eyes and, once again, place one hand on your chest and the other on your stomach. As you breathe in, visualize yourself flattening your diaphragm by pushing out your lower ribs. Feel the air being drawn deeper and deeper into your lungs. As you do so, you will notice a slight increase of pressure against your lower back and the chair. As you breathe out, consciously pull in your abdominal muscles, if necessary using your hand to push down your stomach.

If you have any difficulty doing this, place both hands, fingertips touching, on your stomach. When your diaphragm flattens, notice how the fingertips separate as your stomach, sides and back expand. Such deep, abdominal breathing infuses your blood with extra oxygen and triggers the release of endorphins which lift your mood, making you feel far more confident and positive about the challenges of the day ahead.

Start each working day with thirty seconds of abdominal breathing. You will find that it clears your head and relaxes your body, putting you in an ideal mental and physical state to start the day's work.

MAKING YOUR BRAIN MORE ALERT

After working at mentally demanding tasks for a while, the brain may become sluggish. Regain lost alertness by means of an ancient form of breathing known in yoga as sun–moon or alternate-nostril breathing.

The inside of the nose is covered with a spongy lining that is rich in erectile tissue which constantly swells and shrinks. As this tissue expands in one nostril it decreases in the other, following a cycle which reverses every 95 to 120 minutes. This means that we always have either a right- or left-dominant airflow.

When the air is flowing mainly through the right nostril we tend to be active, aggressive, alert and orientated towards the outside world. When the air is flowing mainly through the left nostril we are in a quieter, more receptive frame of mind and we are intuitive and inwardly directed. Research suggests that airflow through the right nostril stimulates the internal organs towards more active states, such as digesting food.

To check which of your nostrils is open and active right now, simply close one by pressing against it with a fingertip, and inhale through the other. Now swap over and see which nostril allows the air to pass up it more easily. If you check again in an hour or so from now, you will probably find that the other nostril is now fully open and allows air to flow easily.

Sun–moon or alternate-nostril breathing is designed to restore the balance between right- and left-brain function. (If you have difficulty sleeping, carry out this exercise immediately before going to bed. Its calming effect helps to ensure a good night's rest.)

1. Sit comfortably, with your head and neck fairly straight. Breathe slowly and gently, consciously using your diaphragm.
2. Press your right thumb gently against your right nostril and slowly breathe out.
3. Inhale.
4. Lift your thumb to open the right nostril, then press the middle finger of your right hand against your left nostril.

5. Slowly exhale.
6. Now inhale through your left nostril.
7. Repeat this sequence, inhaling and exhaling a total of three times through each nostril.
8. Go through the whole sequence twice more, breathing normally between each round. This makes a total of nine complete breaths through each nostril.

Practise every evening before going to sleep.

REVITALIZING MIND AND BODY

This final exercise may be done while standing, but you will probably find it easier if you sit down and close your eyes. Start with your arms hanging straight down at your sides. Take a deep breath and feel your chest expanding as you bring your arms around in front of you and slowly up over your head. As you inhale, imagine clean, pure air filling your body and flooding it with energy. Stretch as you breathe out while slowly bringing your arms down.

Repeat the exercise three times. Feel the warmth of each inhaled breath dissolving away any tensions in mind or body.

SUMMARY

In this chapter I have examined some of the ways in which working in an office can jeopardize your health. While you may not be able to make any significant changes to the workplace, there are simple steps that you can take to reduce some of the more obvious adverse effects.

● Drink eight glasses of water each day to prevent dehydration.
● Try and work by natural light whenever possible. If this is impossible, replace tungsten bulbs in desk lamps with light balanced to reproduce daylight. If this too is impossible, spend at least fifteen minutes a day in the open air.
● Views of grass and trees are beneficial to our health. If this is not possible, try to take at least one walk a day in a park or garden. If all else fails, pot plants on or near your desk could help.

- Use an ionizer to counter the effects of positive ions produced by many electronic devices found around the office, as well as by synthetic fabrics.
- Use the three simple breathing techniques described in order to banish stress and to increase alertness.

11   Surviving Overload

'Our life is frittered away by detail. Simplify, simplify.'
Henry David Thoreau, *Where I Lived, And What I Lived For*

In 1987, a major British building society called in the Serious Fraud Office: they suspected an employee had embezzled a large amount of money from them by means of an elaborate and extremely complex fraud. After two years spent closely examining the society's database, the SFO officials finally traced the source of the fraud and arrested the culprit.

Curious to know whether computer software could have speeded up this time-consuming investigation, the database was passed to a team of experts in a field known as 'data mining'. Their computer took just three days to discover a pattern of fraud the investigating officers had needed 730 days to find.

At a speed unprecedented in any other field of technology in human history, computers have become our most potent and important tool – modern society certainly could not manage without them. Yet the extent of their contribution to our lives remains open to question. Where computers can and do excel is in storing, retrieving and analysing virtually unlimited quantities of data with unrivalled speed and precision.

From my warnings and comments in this book, you may have been left with two impressions. The first is that, far from being a 'dangerous thing', as Alexander Pope suggested, 'a little learning' is preferable to extensive knowledge. The second is that all decision-making and problem-solving should be left to a series of logical procedures that provide no role for intuition, insight or gut reactions.

If this is your impression, then I apologize, for nothing could be further from what was intended. I am certainly not suggesting that 'when ignorance is bliss, 'tis folly to be wise'. All decisions and problem-solving depend on having the greatest and most feasible amount of *relevant* and *reliable* information on the subject.

What I *am* arguing is that, since the potential amount of information available on almost any topic is now so vast, one cannot continue digging for data indefinitely. The time must come – and often sooner than later – when you have to call a halt for a moment and apply thought and action to what has been discovered.

All solutions to complex problems are never more than partial; they are subject to change, or even to complete reversal, as new knowledge comes to light. It is also true that ploughing through data is tiring. The more data you process, the more fatigued you become, and, unless care is taken, that fatigue can lead to serious health problems.

None of the procedures I have described in this book for reading and learning more efficiently, for solving problems and making decisions more effectively, are tools that can be applied in a mindless or mechanical way. Each demands an insight into the nature of the challenge, in terms of the relevance or irrelevance of the information selected. What they can and will do is enable you to

- get a clear and objective grasp of the situation
- peel away layers of needless complexity and arrive at the very heart of the matter
- dissect and expose the building-blocks of problems
- identify and explore all the options available when making decisions.

In order to survive information overload and significantly reduce the risk to mental and physical well-being, we need to follow the following six rules:

Rule 1: Know Only What You Need to Know

When acquiring information for business or professional purposes, do so on a 'need to know' basis; that is, seek out only what you actually 'need' for the task at hand. Do not be led astray down side-avenues and into minor issues, no matter how attractive or intriguing they may seem. Before reading or learning any new information, test it against the Usefulness Index.

- How relevant is it?
- How reliable is it?
- How hard will it be to access the required information from that particular source?
- What purpose is being served by acquiring this data? How will you use it?

If information fails this test for any reason, then ignore it. Do not take the time, trouble and effort to acquire knowledge just for the sake of it. Your brain's capacity for directed attention is strictly limited.

After a while, mental fatigue will set in. Think of this capacity as fuel in a car. Clearly, you can travel only so far without running dry. What the wise business motorist does is to make the most profitable use of those energy reserves, rather than squandering it on purposeless jaunts. The wise information worker adopts exactly the same approach. He or she knows that info-junk, whether in printed or electronic form, clogs the mind as effectively as junk foods lead to intestinal blockages.

Rule 2: Spend Time Browsing

While Rule 1 should always be followed, creative thinking demands that we introduce a measure of serendipity into knowledge acquisition. What the brain does best is to make connections, identify links and find novel pathways between apparently unconnected and disparate items.

Perhaps the most famous example of serendipity in action was Archimedes' discovery while in the bath that the volume of overflow was exactly equal to the bulk of that portion of his body he had placed in the water. This caused him, so legend has it, to run naked through the streets of Syracuse shouting '*Eureka*' – 'I have found it'. Applying the same principle, he was able to measure the amount of gold used in the crown of his friend, King Hiero, and so prove that the crooked goldsmith had adulterated it.

Serendipity later played a role in discoveries such as some of those made in photography, organic chemistry, the invention of artificial fabrics, vaccinations, antibiotics, X-ray, nuclear fission and the discovery of America.[1]

Always build an element of serendipity into your thought processes. Spend spare moments skimming and scanning a variety of information sources not directly connected to your main line of work. Be an eclectic collector of 'unconsidered trifles' and squirrel them away, either in your mind or in some better-organized reference system, for future use. Adopt a playful approach to novel information, toss it around inside your head and allow yourself to form free associations and see where the journey leads to.

One highly creative university scientist I know sets aside twenty minutes at the end of each day to browse through journals unconnected with her own area of expertise. During this time she dips in and out of a dozen or more articles, with no particular plan or pattern to her reading. She says – and I can confirm this from personal experience – that the mind has a tendency to focus in on items which are, or may be, relevant to current problems and decisions.

Try this for yourself. Flick through magazines and newspapers, take down books at random and cast an eye over them, pay attention to odds-and-ends of information in your daily surroundings. But always do so in a relaxed and unhurried manner. This may seem like the antithesis of 'reading with a purpose', whose importance I have constantly emphasized. In fact, there is a clear purpose for such sauntering through the realms of seemingly irrelevant information. That purpose is to spark insights and intuitions, to provide your brain with the material for creative thinking about tasks directly related to the business or profession you are in. To get a good idea, you need to get lots of ideas. Serendipity will help those ideas to flow freely.

Rule 3: Build Your Metaknowledge

Metaknowledge is the knowledge of where to find things. These days this is one of the most important skills any information gatherer can bring to his or her daily challenges. In this, as in most mentally demanding tasks, storing such information outside memory is far better, safer and more efficient than trying to keep such links in your mind. Use a software package, such as Endnote©, to maintain an easily searched-through library of sources. The more links you can make into such systems, the easier it will be to access the required references quickly and easily.

Rule 4: Use Fast, Effective Search Engines

In the future, the most competitive and successful companies will be those that are first to adopt search-and-retrieval software and the first to implement strategies for organizing information for future use. Internal databases (Intranets) should be an information repository freely available to anyone within the organization; this will ensure that knowledge is neither misplaced nor hoarded. These Intranets should always have access to relevant third-party information providers, to ensure that they are as relevant to employees' needs as possible.

In a recent study, which I conducted on behalf of Financial Times Profile, we found that the amount of data described as infojunk (calculated using the relevance × reliability/ease of access formula) was 34 per cent on Intranets without an outside service provider, but fell to 15 per cent for those whose system was open to external information sources.

When surfing the Net for information, always use the search engine most appropriate to the task.

Rule 5: Don't Panic

As I explained in Chapter Nine, having to make difficult decisions – or solve intricate problems – against the clock can lead to the unhelpful mental states of defensive avoidance or hyper-vigilance. Avoid these by allowing yourself, whenever possible, sufficient time to reflect on the situation and apply one or more of the techniques described in this book. When this is not possible, keep in mind the various traps and sources of biased thinking that I have outlined. Knowing your own decision-making style should help you to identify those situations in which your style is likely either to strengthen or to undermine your ability to think rationally about the situation.

Rule 6: Rationalize and Control Communications

Much of the stress of information overload could be eliminated by a more sensible and rational approach to the communication of information within large organizations. In some companies, for example, e-mail memos are routinely copied to hundreds – even thousands – of employees, not because the information is relevant to them, but as a power play used by managers to establish their position in the hierarchy.

Another increasing cause of stress and overload is the rise of hostile e-mails known as 'flames'. Based on a catch-phrase of The Human Torch, a character in the Marvel comics, flames first appeared on Internet bulletin boards but can now be found in large numbers on internal company Nets. Flames range from sexually or racially offensive comments to personal attacks designed to hurt and humiliate. 'Shared flames' are criticisms sent not only to the person concerned but also to all their colleagues. The use of flames seems to be on the increase. In research I conducted recently, more than half the managers questioned reported being victims.[2]

Flames are not just a high-tech weapon for the office bully; often they are the response of a chronically stressed manager striving to meet impossibly tight deadlines. In the past, poor performance or foolish mistakes by a subordinate might have been dealt with by talking to the offender and finding out what had gone wrong. Workplace pressures now lead many bosses to using e-mail flames as a quick fix. As one respondent put it: 'Managers never have time to talk you through a problem or explain what you should be doing differently. They'd rather just blast off a nasty e-mail telling you to pull your socks up.'

All of this points to a growing alienation among employees, and between managers and their subordinates, and is one of the most worrying consequences of a decline in face-to-face communications. Organizations should take a number of steps to benefit from advances in technology, while avoiding their potential pitfalls.

- Workers at all levels should be trained to listen! Contrary to popular belief, listening is not a skill that comes naturally, but something that has to be learnt and practised.
- Face-to-face meetings should be organized on a regular basis, rather than messages being transmitted electronically. These need not be a formal, agenda-style get-together but informal discussions and conversations, around the coffee machine or in the staff canteen. Some large American companies are now creating areas with easy chairs and a relaxed décor in which staff can come together for such meetings. During a recent study I conducted among more than a thousand UK

employees,[3] the overwhelming majority of employees (91 per cent) believed that 'office lounges' would also significantly boost their creativity.

- Managers should avoid using e-mail for criticizing, advising or guiding employees. All of these functions require face-to-face discussions.
- Companies should reduce resentment by having formal channels for dealing with flame-mail offences.
- The role played by communications abuses in increasing workplace stress and information overload should be recognized and dealt with.

There is every reason to suppose that the amount of information being generated and communicated is going to increase significantly in the foreseeable future. Unless steps are taken, at both personal and corporate levels, to tackle the threats to the well-being such information overload poses, then individuals and the organizations employing them will be the losers. Already we are seeing the damaging results of infoglut, not merely on the mental and physical health of information workers but also on their motivation, morale and productivity.

The human brain is an awe-inspiringly complex and marvellous biochemical machine, which is capable of tasks that computers seem unlikely ever to achieve. But, like all sensitive and delicate items of equipment, it has its limitations and weaknesses. Brains do not take kindly to being under great pressure for any extended length of time; they need rest, they need relaxation, and they need a balance in the tasks they are asked to perform.

Unlike microchips, they have a powerful emotional component. Indeed, it has been argued that this emotional element is far more powerful and more important than our intellectual powers; it may well colour our judgements and inform our choices to an extent that is still not fully appreciated. Unless the emotional quotient of information workers, their EQ, is taken into account to the same extent as their IQ, then systems – at both personal and organization level – must fail.

In this book I have described some of the ways the brain copes, or fails to cope, with the challenges of a world in which information has become a holy grail. It is not a matter of *whether* we should develop new ways of thinking about and dealing with information overload; just how quickly we are able to do so. As Humpty Dumpty put it in *Through the Looking-Glass*, the question is 'which is to be master – that's all'.

Notes

Introduction

1. Reuters. 1997. *Dying for Information. An Investigation into the Effects of Information Overload in the UK and Worldwide.* London: Reuters Business Information.
2. Study for Pitney Bowes, conducted by Gallup and the Institute for the Future. 1998.

Chapter One

1. In Lewis Carroll's *Through the Looking Glass* the Red Queen warns: 'Now, *here*, you see, it takes all the running *you* can do, to keep in the same place. If you want to get somewhere else, you must run at least twice as fast as that!'
2. Siegel, M. 1998. 'Do Computers Slow Us Down?', *Fortune*, 30 March, pp. 18–19.
3. Alsop, S. 1997. 'Can Computers Help You Think? No', *Fortune*, 28 April, pp. 192–4.

Chapter Two

1. Forsythe, J. 1998. 'E-Business Ahead', *Newsweek*, 23 March. US Congress, Office of Technology Assessment, 1986. (The OTA Report) *Intellectual Property Rights in an Age of Electronics and Innovation* (OTA-CIT-302): 32–3.
2. Wurman, R. S. 1989. *Information Anxiety.* London: Pan.
3. Bateson, G. 1973. *Steps to an Ecology of Mind.* St Albans: Paladin, p. 242.
4. Grossberg, S. 1992. *Studies of Mind and Brain.* Cambridge, Massachusetts: MIT Press.
5. Davenport, T. H., and Prusak, L. 1998. *Working Knowledge: How Organizations Manage What They Know.* Boston: Harvard Business School Press, p. xii.
6. Dertouzos, M. 1997. *What Will Be.* London: Piatkus.

7. Drucker, P. F. 1988. 'The Coming of the New Organisation', *Harvard Business Review* 66 (January–February): 45–53.

8. In Davenport and Prusak, *Working Knowledge*, p. xii.

Chapter Three

1. Wallich, P. 1998. 'Preserving the Word', *Scientific American*, January 1988.

2. Shaughnessy, A. F., Slawson, D. C., and Bennett, J. H. 1994. 'Becoming an information master: a guidebook to the medical information jungle', *The Journal of Family Practice*, 39(5) (Nov.).

3. Safir, W. 1997. *Good Advice on Writing*, by William and Leonard Safir. Cited in *Forbes*, 29 December 1997, p. 32.

Chapter Four

1. Waddington, C. H. 1977. *Tools for Thought.* London: Jonathan Cape.

2. Naisbitt, J. 1984. *Megatrends.* London: Macdonald and Co.

3. De Solla Price is quoted in Waddington, *Tools for Thought*, p. 34.

4. Lukasiewicz, J. 1972. *The Ignorance Explosion*, trans. New York. Acad. Sci., p. 373.

5. Reuters. 1997. *The Reuters Guide to Good Information Strategy.* London. p. 8.

6. Wolfe, J. M. 1997. 'In a blink of the mind's eye', *Nature*, 387, 19 June, pp. 756–7. Wolfe was discussing two papers in the same issue: Joseph, J. S., Chun, M. M. and Nakayama, K. 1997. 'Attentional requirements in a "preattentive" feature search task'. *Nature*, 387, 19 June, pp. 805–7; and Duncan, J., Martens, S. and Ward, R. 1997. 'Restricted attentional capacity within but not between sensory modalities'. *Nature*, 387, 19 June, pp. 808–10.

7. McCarthy, B. 1980. *The 4-Mat System.* Illinois: Excell Inc.

8. Pask, G. 1976. 'Styles and strategies of learning', *British Journal of Educational Psychology*, 46: 128–48.

9. Kelly, K. 1998. 'The Third Culture', *Science*, 279, 13 February, pp. 992–3.

10. Locke, J. 1690. *Essay concerning Human Understanding. The Quarterly Review* [1854].

11. Credited to Samuel Foote by Maria Edgeworth, *Harry and Lucy Concluded* [1825] vol. II. As a footnote (no pun intended) to history, the Great Panjandrum of his nonsense prose was taken by British military inventors during the Second World War and given to a fearsome device consisting of two giant wheels carrying an explosive charge. This was intended to blast through German defensive positions following the D-Day landings.

12. Collins, A. M., and Quillian, M. R. 1972. 'How to Make a Language User',

Organization of Memory, eds E. Tulving and W. Donaldson. New York: Academic Press.

13. Atkinson, R. C. 1957. 'A Stochastic Model for Rote Serial Learning', *Psychometrika*, 22, 87–95; *id*, 1972. 'Ingredients for a Theory of Instruction', *American Psychologist*, 27, 275–89.

14. Lewis, D., and Greene, J. 1982. *Thinking Better*. New York: Henry Holt & Co.

15. Atkinson, R. C. 'A Stochastic Model . . .'

Chapter Five

1. McCrone, J. 1993. *The Myth of Irrationality: The Science of the Mind from Plato to Star Trek*. London: Macmillan.

2. Luria, A. R. 1968. *The Mind of a Mnemonist*. New York: Basic.

3. Gross, R. D. 1994. *Psychology, the Science of Mind and Behaviour*. London: Hodder & Stoughton. 2nd edition, p. 353.

4. Parkin, A. J. 1987. *Memory & Amnesia*. Oxford: Blackwell, p. 54.

5. Pinker, S. 1998. *How the Mind Works*. London: Allen Lane, The Penguin Press.

6. Miller, G. A. 1956. 'The magical number seven, plus or minus two: some limits on our capacity for processing information', *Psychological Review*, 63: 81–97.

7. Erdelyi, M., and Kleinbard, J. 1987. 'Has Ebbinghaus decayed with time?: the growth of recall (Hypermnesia) over days', *Journal of Experimental Psychology* 4: 275–89.

8. Baddeley, A. 1983. *Your Memory: a User's Guide*. London: Penguin, p. 44.

Chapter Six

1. Janis, I. L. 1982. 'Decision Making Under Stress', in L. Goldberger and S. Breznitz (eds.), *Handbook of Stress. Theoretical and Clinical Aspects*. New York: Free Press.

2. ibid., p. 75.

3. ibid., pp. 72–3.

4. Wickelgren, W. A. 1974. *How to Solve Problems: Elements of a Theory of Problems and Problem-Solving*. San Francisco: W. H. Freeman & Co.

5. Josh Billings (Henry Wheeler Shaw). 1874. *Encyclopaedia of Wit and Wisdom*.

6. Goldratt, E. M., and Cox, J. *The Goal*. 1989. Aldershot: Gower, pp. 116–17.

Chapter Seven

1. Duncker, K. 'On Problem Solving', *Psychological Monographs* 270 (1945).

2. Interview with George Miller, *Psychology Today*, 1980.

Chapter Eight

1. Janis, I. L., and Mann, L. 1977. *Decision Making: A psychological analysis of conflict, choice, and commitment.* New York: Free Press.
2. Janis. 'Decision Making Under Stress'.
3. DeJesus, E. X. 1998. 'Year 2000 Survival Guide', *Byte*, July, pp. 52–62.
4. Mandel, M. J., *et al.* 1998. 'Zap! How the Year 2000 bug will hurt the economy', *Business Week.* 2 March, pp. 47–51.
5. Janis. 'Decision Making Under Stress', pp. 69–87.
6. Dr Jonathan Koehle, cited in: P. Aldhous (1998) 'What chance we've got the wrong man?', *New Scientist*, 28 February, No. 2123, p. 20.
7. Matthews, R. 1997. 'How right can you be?', *New Scientist*, 8 March, No. 2072 28–31.
8. Lewis and Greene, *Thinking Better.*
9. After expelling Tom Brown (1663–1704), Dr John Fell, Dean of Christ Church (1625–86), offered to take him back if Brown was able to translate the 33rd *Epigram* of Martial: *Non amo te, Zabidi, nec possum dicere quare: Hoc tantum possum dicere non amo te.* The mocking verse was his student's response to this offer.
10. Stoner, J., 1968. 'Risky and cautious shifts in group decisions: the influence of widely held values', *Journal of Experimental Social Psychology*, 4: 442–59.
11. Neumann, J. von, and Morgenstern, O. 1947. *Theory of Games and Economic Behaviour.* Princeton, New Jersey: Princeton University Press.
12. Swalm, R. O., 1983. 'Utility Theory – Insights Into Risk Taking', in D. N. Dixon (ed.), *Using Logical Techniques for Making Better Decisions.* New York: John Wiley & Sons, Inc.

Chapter Nine

1. Graves, D., and Lethbridge, D. 1975. 'Could Decision Analysis have Saved Hamlet?', *Journal of Management Studies*, 12: 216–24.

Chapter Ten

1. Batmanghelidj, F. 1994. 'Your Body's many cries for Water', *The Therapist Ltd.*
2. Guyton, A. C. 1976. 'Regulation on Blood Volume', in *Textbook of Medical Physiology*, 5th edition. W. B. Saunders Company: Philadelphia, p. 479.
3. Best, A. S. 1976. 'Pan American World Airways Air Conditioning Tests During Revenue Flights', Boeing Reports No. T6-4453-B747SP. Reprinted in *Aviation, Space and Environmental Medicine*, 2/80, p. 170.

4. Irwin, M. 1992. 'Jet Lag Afflicts Many But Few Know the Cure', cited in D. Fairechild (1992), *Jet Smart*, Berkeley, California: Flyana Rhyme Inc.

5. Sharma, V. M., Sridharan, K., Pichan, G., and Panwar, M. W. 1986. 'Influence of heat-stress induced dehydration on mental functions', *Ergonomics*, vol. 29(6) (June), 791-9.

6. Krueger, A. P. 1977. *The Ion Effect*. London: Bantam.

7. Elanra Ioniser – Bionic Products Pty Ltd, The White House, 63 Manly Drive, Robina, Queensland 4226.

8. Murray-Bruce, D. J. 1990. *Promoting Employee Health*. London: Macmillan.

9. Kaplan, R., and Kaplan, S. 1989. *The Experience of Nature: A Psychological Perspective*. Cambridge University Press. Cambridge.

10. ibid.

11. Southard, D. R., Coates, T. J., Kolodner, K., Parker, F. et al. 1986. 'Relationship between mood and blood pressure in the natural environment: An adolescent population', *Health Psychology* (5): 469–80.

Chapter Eleven

1. Roberts, R. M. 1989. *Serendipity. Accidental Discoveries in Science*. New York: John Wiley and Sons.

2. Research conducted on behalf of Novel software, 1998.

3. Research conducted on behalf of IKEA, 1998.

Bibliography

Alsop, S. (1997), 'Can Computers Help You Think? No', *Fortune*, 28 April, pp. 192–4.

Alter, S. (1996), *Information Systems*, The Benjamin/Cummings Publishing Company, Inc., New York.

Baddeley, A. (1990), *Human Memory: Theory and Practice*, Lawrence Erlbaum Associates, Hove, Sussex.

Baron, J. (1985), *Rationality and Intelligence*, Cambridge University Press, Cambridge.

Beaver, D. (1994), *Lazy Learning*, Element, Shaftesbury, Dorset.

Bessen, J. (1993), 'Riding the marketing information wave', *Harvard Business Review*, September–October (Vol. 71, No. 5), pp. 150–60.

Bransford, J. D., and Stein, B. S. (1993) (2nd edn), *The Ideal Solver*, Freeman, Oxford.

Brod, C. (1984), *Techno Stress*, Addison-Wesley Publishing Company, London.

Brown, W. (1992), 'Lies, damn lies and government statistics', *New Scientist*, 5 December, No. 1850, pp. 13–14.

Buchwald, D., *et al.* (1992), 'A chronic illness characterized by fatigue, neurologic and immunologic disorders and active human herpesvirus type 6 infection', *Annals Internal Medicine*, 116: 103–12.

Chafetz, M. D. (1992), *Smart for Life: How to Improve Your Brain Power at Any Age*, Penguin, London.

Claxton, G. (1997), *Hare Brain, Tortoise Mind*, Fourth Estate, London.

Conners, M. (1997), *Race to the Intelligent State*, Capstone, Oxford.

Davenport, T. H. (1994), 'Saving IT's soul: human-centred information management', *Harvard Business Review*, Vol. 72(2).

Davenport, T. H., and Prusak, L. (1998), *Working Knowledge: How Organizations Manage What They Know*, Harvard Business School Press, Boston, Massachusetts.

Davidson, C. (1993), 'What your database hides away', *New Scientist*, 9 January, No. 1855.

De Bono, E. (1994), *Parallel Thinking*, Viking, London.

DeLuca, J., Johnson, S. K., and Natelson, B. H. (1993), 'Information processing efficiency in chronic fatigue syndrome and multiple sclerosis', *Arch. Neurol.* 50: 301–4.

Dertouzos, M. (1997), *What Will Be*, Piatkus, London.

Dixon, D. N. (ed.) (1983), *Using Logical Techniques for Making Better Decisions*, John Wiley & Sons, Inc., New York.

Drucker, P. F. (1995), 'The Information Executives Truly Need', *Harvard Business Review*, January–February, Vol. 73, No. 1, pp. 54–62.

Dudley, G. A. (1986), *Double Your Learning Power*, Thorson, London.

Duncan, J., Martens, S., and Ward, R. (1997), 'Restricted attentional capacity within but not between sensory modalities', *Nature*, Vol. 387, 19 June, pp. 808–10.

Earl, M. J. (1996), *Information Management*, Oxford University Press, New York.

Economist, The (1996), *Going Digital*, Profile Books, London.

Gates, B. (1995), *The Road Ahead*, Penguin, London.

George, F. H. (1980), *Problem Solving*, Duckworth, London.

Gibbs, W. W. (1997), 'Taking Computers To Task', *Scientific American*, July, pp. 64–71.

Greenfield, S. (1997), *The Human Brain: A Guided Tour*, Weidenfeld & Nicolson, London.

Hayes, J. R. (1981), *The Complete Problem Solver*, The Franklin Institute Press, Philadelphia.

Hickie, I., Lloyd, A., and Wakefield, D. (1991), 'Chronic fatigue syndrome and depression', *Lancet*, 337: 992.

Holderness, M. (1992), 'Time to shelve the library?', *New Scientist*, 5 December, No. 1850, pp. 22–3.

Joseph, J. S., Chun, M. M., and Nakayama, K. (1997), 'Attentional requirements in a preattentive feature search task', *Nature*, Vol. 387, 19 June, pp. 805–7.

Kaplan, R. (1975), 'Some methods and strategies in the prediction of preference', *Landscape Assessment: Values, Perceptions and Resources*, F. H. Zube, (eds), Dowden, Hutchinson & Ross, Stroudsburg, Pennsylvania.

Kaplan, R. (1977), 'Preference and everyday nature: method and application', *Psychological Perspectives on Environment and Behaviour: Theory, Research and Application*, D. Stokols (ed.), Plenum, New York.

Kaplan, R. (1983), 'The role of nature in the urban context', *Human Behaviour and Environment: Advances in Theory and Research*, I. Altman and J. F. Wohwill (eds.), Plenum, New York.

Kaplan, R., and Herbert, E. J. (1987), 'Cultural and subcultural comparisons in preferences for natural settings', *Landscape and Urban Planning*, 14: 281–93.

Kaplan, S. (1972), 'The challenge of environmental psychology: a proposal for a new functionalism', *American Psychologist*, 27: 141–3.

Kaplan, S. (1973), 'Cognitive maps in perception and thought', *Image and Environment: Cognitive Mapping and Spatial Behaviour*, R. M. Downs and D. Stea (eds), Aldine, Chicago.

Kaplan, S. (1975), 'An informal model for the prediction of preference', *Landscape Assessment*, Dowden, Hutchinson & Ross, Stroudsburg, Pennsylvania.

Kaplan, S. (1976), 'Adaptation, structure and knowledge', *Environmental Knowing: Theories, Research and Methods*, G. T. Moore and R. G. Golledye (eds), Dowden, Hutchinson & Ross, Stroudsburg, Pennsylvania.

Kaplan, S. (1978), 'Attention and fascination: The search for cognitive clarity', *Humanscape: Environments for People*, S. Kaplan and R. Kaplan (eds), Duxbury, North Scituate, Massachusetts.

Kaplan, S. (1987), 'Aesthetics, effect and cognition: Environmental preferences from an evolutionary perspective', *Environment and Behaviour*, 19: 332.

Kaplan, S., Kaplan, R., and Wendt, J. S., (1972), 'Rated preferences and complexity for natural and urban visual material', *Perception and Psychophysics*, 12: 354–6.

Kaplan, S., and Wendt, J. S. (1972), 'Preference and the visual environment: complexity and some alternatives', *Environmental Design: Research and Practice*, W. J. Mitchell (ed.), Dowden, Hutchinson & Ross, Stroudsburg, Pennsylvania.

Katz, R., (1984), 'Empowerment and synergy: Expanding the community's healing resources', *Prevention in Human Sciences*, 3: 201–26.

Korner, T. W. (1996), *The Pleasures of Counting*, Cambridge University Press, Cambridge.

Lane, R. E. (1991), *The Market Experience*, Cambridge University Press, Cambridge.

Leigh, A. (1983), *Decisions, Decisions!*, The Institute of Personnel Management, London.

Leutwyler, K. (1997), 'Profile: Michael L. Dertouzos', *Scientific American*, July, pp. 19–22.

Lewis, H. W. (1997), *Why Flip a Coin?: The Art and Science of Good Decisions*, John Wiley & Sons, Inc., Chichester.

Lynch, C. (1997), 'Searching the Internet', *Scientific American*, March, pp. 44–8.

Matthews, R. (1996), 'Panning for Data', *New Scientist*, 25 May, pp. 30–33.

Matthews, R. (1997), 'How right can you be?', *New Scientist*, 8 March, No. 2072, pp. 28–31.

Mayer, J. J. (1995), *Time Management for Dummies: Briefcase Edition*, IDG Books, Foster City, California.

McCrone, J. (1993), *The Myth of Irrationality: The Science of the Mind from Plato to Star Trek*, Macmillan, London.

McKie, A. (1994), 'International Research in a Relative World', *Journal of the Market Research Society*, Vol. 38, No. 1.

McPherson, P. K. (1995), 'Information Mastery', *Managing Information*, June, 2: 6, pp. 33–6.

Midgley, M. (1989), *Wisdom, Information and Wonder*, Routledge, London.

Moody, P. E. (1983), *Decision Making: Proven Methods for Better Decisions*, McGraw-Hill, London.

Mullins, J. (1995), 'All wired up and raring to go', *New Scientist*, 5 August, Vol. 147, No. 1989, pp. 30–34.

Nash, T. (1997) (ed.), *Managing Your Messages Effectively*, The Director Publications Ltd, London.

Negroponte, N. (1995), *Being Digital*, Hodder & Stoughton, London.

Norman, D. A. (1993), *Things that make us smart*, Addison-Wesley, New York.

Novak, J. D., and Gowin, D. B. (1984), *Learning How to Learn*, Cambridge University Press, Cambridge.

Oaksford, M. (1997), 'Thinking and the rational analysis of human reasoning', *The Psychologist*, June, Vol. 10, No. 6, pp. 257–60.

Plotkin, H. (1994), *Darwin Machines and the Nature of Knowledge*, Penguin, London.

Pokras, S. (1989), *Systematic Problem-Solving and Decision-Making*, Kogan Page, London.

Polya, G. (1957) (2nd edn), *How to Solve It*, Doubleday Anchor Books, New York.

Pritchett, P. (1994), *New Work Habits for a Radically Changing World: 13 Ground Rules for Job Success in the Information Age*, Pritchett & Associates, Inc., Washington, UK.

Ratan, S. (1995), 'Snail Mail Struggles to Survive', *Time*: Special Issue, Spring, p. 36.

Rochlin, G. I. (1997), *Trapped in the Net*, Princeton University Press, Princeton, New Jersey.

Sagan, C. (1996), *The Demon-Haunted World: Science as a Candle in the Dark*, Headline, London.

Saxby, S. (1990), *The Age of Information*, The Macmillan Press Ltd, London.

Schatz, B. R. (1997), 'Information retrieval in digital libraries: bringing search to the net', *Science*, Vol. 275, 17 January, pp. 327–34.

Sherman, M. (1997), *Why People Believe Weird Things*, W. H. Freeman & Co., New York.

Skyrme, D. (1994), 'Ten Ways to Add Value to Your Business', *Managing Information*, March, 1: 3, pp. 20–24.

Souttar, J. (1995), 'Designing Information for On-Screen Display', *Managing Information*, March, 2: 3, pp. 23–4.

Stewart, T. A. (1997), 'Brain Power: Who Owns It . . . How They Profit from It', *Fortune*, 17 March, pp. 65–8.

Thouless, R. H. (1953), *Straight and Crooked Thinking*, Pan, London.

Treacy, D. (1997), 'Out with the in-tray', *Director*, January, pp. 40–43.

Tullett, A. D. (1995), 'The adaptive-innovative (A-I) cognitive styles of male and female project managers: some implications for the management of change', *Journal of Occupational and Organizational Psychology*, 68, 359–65.

Turkle, S. (1995), *Life on the Screen: Identity in the Age of the Internet*, Phoenix, London.

Warr, P. (ed.) (1996), *Psychology at Work* (4th edn), Penguin, London.

Wolfe, J. M. (1997), 'In a blink of the mind's eye', *Nature*, Vol. 387, 19 June, pp. 756–7.

Wurman, R. S. (1989), *Information Anxiety*, Pan, London.

Index

Numbers in italics refer to Figures.

READ MORE IN PENGUIN

In every corner of the world, on every subject under the sun, Penguin represents quality and variety – the very best in publishing today.

For complete information about books available from Penguin – including Puffins, Penguin Classics and Arkana – and how to order them, write to us at the appropriate address below. Please note that for copyright reasons the selection of books varies from country to country.

In the United Kingdom: Please write to *Dept. EP, Penguin Books Ltd, Bath Road, Harmondsworth, West Drayton, Middlesex UB7 0DA*

In the United States: Please write to *Consumer Sales, Penguin Putnam Inc., P.O. Box 12289 Dept. B, Newark, New Jersey 07101-5289*. VISA and MasterCard holders call 1-800-788-6262 to order Penguin titles

In Canada: Please write to *Penguin Books Canada Ltd, 10 Alcorn Avenue, Suite 300, Toronto, Ontario M4V 3B2*

In Australia: Please write to *Penguin Books Australia Ltd, P.O. Box 257, Ringwood, Victoria 3134*

In New Zealand: Please write to *Penguin Books (NZ) Ltd, Private Bag 102902, North Shore Mail Centre, Auckland 10*

In India: Please write to *Penguin Books India Pvt Ltd, 11 Community Centre, Panchsheel Park, New Delhi 110017*

In the Netherlands: Please write to *Penguin Books Netherlands bv, Postbus 3507, NL-1001 AH Amsterdam*

In Germany: Please write to *Penguin Books Deutschland GmbH, Metzlerstrasse 26, 60594 Frankfurt am Main*

In Spain: Please write to *Penguin Books S. A., Bravo Murillo 19, 1° B, 28015 Madrid*

In Italy: Please write to *Penguin Italia s.r.l., Via Benedetto Croce 2, 20094 Corsico, Milano*

In France: Please write to *Penguin France, Le Carré Wilson, 62 rue Benjamin Baillaud, 31500 Toulouse*

In Japan: Please write to *Penguin Books Japan Ltd, Kaneko Building, 2-3-25 Koraku, Bunkyo-Ku, Tokyo 112*

In South Africa: Please write to *Penguin Books South Africa (Pty) Ltd, Private Bag X14, Parkview, 2122 Johannesburg*

READ MORE IN PENGUIN

BUSINESS AND ECONOMICS

Webonomics   Evan I. Schwartz

In *Webonomics*, Evan I. Schwartz defines nine essential principles for growing your business on the Web. Using case studies of corporations such as IBM and Volvo, as well as smaller companies and web-based start-ups, Schwartz documents both the tremendous failures and the successes on the Web in a multitude of industries.

Inside Organizations   Charles B. Handy

Whatever we do, whatever our profession, organizing is a part of our lives. This book brings together twenty-one ideas which show you how to work with and through other people. There are also questions at the end of each chapter to get you thinking on your own and in a group.

Lloyds Bank Small Business Guide   Sara Williams

This long-running guide to making a success of your small business deals with real issues in a practical way. 'As comprehensive an introduction to setting up a business as anyone could need' *Daily Telegraph*

Teach Yourself to Think   Edward de Bono

Edward de Bono's masterly book offers a structure that broadens our ability to respond to and cope with a vast range of situations. *Teach Yourself to Think* is software for the brain, turning it into a successful thinking mechanism, and, as such, will prove of immense value to us all.

The Road Ahead   Bill Gates

Bill Gates – the man who built Microsoft – takes us back to when he dropped out of Harvard to start his own software company and discusses how we stand on the brink of a new technology revolution that will for ever change and enhance the way we buy, work, learn and communicate with each other.

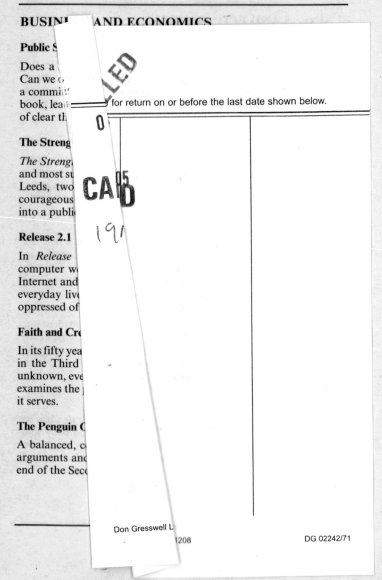

for return on or before the last date shown below.

Don Gresswell L

1208

DG 02242/71